Stacks

...Still Pimpin' In The Game

OG STACK$

Stacks Still... pimpin' in the Game Copyright © 2015 by OG STACK$.

All rights reserved. Printed in the United States of America. No part of this book may be used or reproduced in any manner whatsoever without written permission except in the case of brief quotations embodied in critical articles or reviews.

This book is a work of partial-fiction. However, names, characters, businesses, organizations, places, events and incidents either are the product of the author's imagination or are used fictitiously. Any resemblance to actual persons, living or dead, events, or locales is entirely coincidental.

For information contact:

info@uptownmediaventures.com
ghettoinkpublications@gmail.com

Book and Cover design by Team Uptown and graphic designer Justin Cramer.

ISBN: 978-1-68121-028-5

First Edition: March, 2015

10 9 8 7 6 5 4 3 2 1

This book is dedicated to my Cliffview Hilltop Family my 10th ward OGs and to Collinwood high & to my Team L.A.U and my new family members of Uptown Media Joint Ventures & to all those that had faith in my writings as well as to all my Haters who said I couldn't do it.

I would like to thank my mother sister Fadiah for the Love she gave me when the streets showed no love and I would like say rest in the highest heaven to my Father Abdus-Shakur. I would like say big ups to my one and only brother Muntasir, to my two Daughters Yasmine and Kiara, to my two sons Khayree and Wali (William), my daughters' mother Kimberly Ali, two sisters Asma and Zhulaika, and my brother from another mother Rico (Chill). Also, I would like to send shout outs to Goodgame (Free My Bleed), all my family and friends, to all those on lock down in the Fed's Leavenworth (B - Upper), Mendez, Marquis, Cuzzo, my New York family, my Detroit family Jammat, and last but not least Carrie.

I would like to thank my typist Samantha Strine for putting the finishing touches on my book, my graphic designer Justin Cramer, and a special thanks to K Kelly McElroy. Let's get this money! And I would like to thank anybody else I forgot.

I told y'all I was going to do it!

Chapters	Page
The Pimps Preamble	
Chapter 1 **Ambush Party**	9
Chapter 2 **Crunchy-Black**	19
Chapter 3 **Set-Up! Angry Dyke Style**	23
Chapter 4 **Back in "H-Town"**	35
Chapter 5 **The "Turn Out"**	49
Chapter 6 **High Roller**	55
Chapter 7 **Dope Fiend**	61
Chapter 8 **The Lock Up and Beat Down**	71
Chapter 9 **Consequences**	83
Chapter 10 **A Hoe Into a Housewife**	91
Chapter 11 **Weezy's Dilemma**	97
Chapter 12 **The Worst Kind of Betrayal**	105
Chapter 13 **The Sting**	115
Chapter 14 **Locked Up Again!**	127
About the Author	131

The Pimp's Preamble

Foolish pimps waste their time and energy on frivolous hoes that keep their pockets empty with weak ass thoughts. Then they complain about the way that they are living their lives - a life which they created in the first place. A "gorilla" pimp is a "weak" ass pimp that is stubborn and refuses to learn the real pimpin' game. They control by force. Real pimpin' is mind over matter for strength is the firm basis on which pimpin' is built upon.

No real pimp can be confronted with the difficulties of a confused hoe; that which he has not the power to meet head on and overcome. There are lessons to be learned by every hoe in order to become a successful hoe. The first lesson is that she must discipline herself to control her speech and speak only when spoken to unless she is speaking about money. Then she must let it be born in the mind that laziness is a disease that can only be cured by clearly having an understanding that procrastination leads to laziness. A hoe must keep a firm, fixed determined mind to do whatever it takes to make and keep her pimp happy.

The first step to doing this is to have dignity about herself. Be proud to be a hoe and be the best hoe that she can be. Realize that being a hoe is not a bad thing to be. Pleasing a man outside of her pimp is the worst thing to do when it comes to doing it for free. Every hoe needs to know that the best things in life do not come free and that a dishonest hoe is a trifling hoe which is a nasty hoe that won't last long in the hoe game. As for every pimp that lives life off of his dick and emotions by thinking with the head in between his legs instead of the head on his shoulders – he will eventually become a tender dick emotional non pimping ass "simp." So to all the real pimps keep a thick dick and stay in motion with an EMONTIONLESS HEART.

PIMP OR DIE!

Chapter 1

Ambush Party

Early Saturday morning, October 22nd, all of Stacks' hoes were dressed and ready to go. They all had on a different style cocaine white body cat suit, by the model Ms. Cat, with red bottom open toe heels. He made them wear matching pink chin-chillas.

They were all looking like a group of sexual nymphos all ready to suck a dick and turn a trick for the right price! Stacks had on a custom made powder blue Italian Brioni suit, with a pair of Italian Fennix navy blue ostrich/alligator ankle boots. He was sporting his five thousand dollar platinum pinky ring. He had on his two-toned white and blue spotted full length chin-chilla with the matching brim.

In one hand he had his custom designed diamond incrusted crown top, with a gold tip cane. In the other hand he had his twenty thousand dollar goblet laced with diamonds around the rim, and diamonds placed all over the outside of the goblet spelling: "Pimpin' Stacks."

Precious, K, Sin, Shakim and Akelia were there to represent and support Stacks in his achievements.

Akelia was so fine, 30-26-40 at 4'11 with jet black hair, seductive eyes that seemed to look right through the clothes on ya back. Her skin was like Tahiry Jose's - silky smooth. She was all ass, pigeon toed, as well as bo-legged. She wore a cream color blouse with a pair of hip hugging Baby Phat jeans and a pair of 6 inch stilettos. Her smile revealed a set of perfectly white teeth, that lit up the darkest night.

Ever since Shakim came to Stacks about Akelia, he would avoid her and ignore her flirtatious ways. Stacks didn't know her baby father personally, but out of respect for the Five Percent Nation he didn't put his pimp hand down too hard on her. He basically kept her around as a high paid dancer. But today she was looking extra "pimpalious."

They all exited the Estate heading towards their rides. LA and his crew were all in place waiting in front of five bullet proof triple black Cadillac limo trucks. Stacks had accumulated a lot of dough throughout the year, making money hand over fist.

"Ain't no money like hoe money! Cause hoe money is fo' show money!" yelled Stacks as he climbed into the first limo truck.

Once inside the truck LA turned and said, "My nigga Stacks if you ain't pimpin then I don't know what pimpin is!"

"Pimpin is what pimpin does, pimpin ain't on me my nigga. Pimpin is runnin' through my muthafuckin blood," he responded.

Then he grabbed his cell phone out of his upper pocket and called his mans Stevie from Party All the Time Entertainment. He picked up on the first ring, "P.A. double T Entertainment, how may I help you?"

"Aye yo son, this is Stacks. I'm headed to Sergio's, are you there yet?" Stacks asked.

"Yeah, no doubt everything is all set up. I got the stage together with the seating arrangements as well. The cable stations are here and ready to roll. The catering service has the food and drinks of Champagne ready as well. Three o'clock is when the first performer will begin," answered Stevie.

"Aight then playa, I'll check you later," Stacks said as he hung up the phone.

They arrived at Sergio's mansion. It was the size of a miniature college. When they pulled up to the gate, security called Sergio to get clearance for Stacks and his crew. LA moved up the driveway, that was the length of a mile, at a slow pace as they were pulling up to the front of the mansion. Sergio was excited to greet his guests. When the limo came to a complete stop, all of Stacks' hoes exited first and to his surprise, Akelia, who had rode in the limo with him, exited the right side, then hurried to open Stacks' door.

She looked at him with a devilish smile as he was getting out of the limo. He leaned in like he was about to kiss her, then whispered in her ear: "It's going to take more than a big butt and a sexy smile for you to be worth my while. Cause pimpin and hoeing is the best thing goin. So make no mistakes this pimp here is nowhere near fake!"

Then Sergio approached Stacks.

"Good afternoon my friend! How are you?" he asked.

"It's all pimpin baby, from sun up to sun down, till the sun comes back up. I keep a smut stuck in a rut! How you doin pimpin?" Stacks replied.

"Buenos, everything is bueno my friend!" Sergio exclaimed.

Stacks introduced everybody, then Sergio lead them into the mansion. Right through to the very back of the mansion, to the two backyards. The first was underneath a dome, where the other yard followed. Each yard had a swimming pool, tennis courts and basketball courts. Under the dome is where he had all the festivities set up. There were women everywhere dressed in bikinis. Sergio had at least a hundred Latino female servants. Stacks and his entourage were seated off to the right, up by the DJ booth. When they sat down, Stacks ordered bottles for all of his tables and Sergio had come over with a platter of Purple Haze. Stacks was seated next to Precious, so he had her roll him a fat spliff.

Sin looked at K with an evil eye from a far as K liked flirting with his woman without any interruptions and Precious was loving it. The cable stations were recording everything from different angles. Stacks signed a contract with one stations allowing them to air the event live and another contract for the other station to show the event at a later date.

A few hours had passed by and the place was filled up with some of the most certified underground people in the world. Stacks even saw that Gorilla Forilla Killa type nigga out of the Bronx, known as Dancer who acquired that name from the streets. They say he'll kill a nigga, show up at the funeral and once the funeral was over and you was six feet in the dirt, he would do some crazy Dominican dance on your grave while drinking on some Barcelon.

As Nonchalant finished his performance, Stacks nodded his head in approval, then looked past him and saw a few of his longtime associates from D.C., known as "Dem Killahs." First there was that fried chicken nigga Cuzzo. Then you had Peat and Repeat Quies and Dee-Blazak. If one didn't kill you, the other one was for sure to kill you. They were professional killers for hire.

"Alright pimps, playas, hoes, gangstas, and macks and everything in between! Today is the day we crown the King of Kings, the pimp of all pimps. It's been a long time coming but the day has finally arrived. Before we go any further please allow me the opportunity to share with ya'll a prerecorded phone call from the inside reaching out. I bring to you all none other than the pantie hoes Unlocka himself, pimpin the mack pimp playa big pimpin Poppa-Locka..." announced the MC.

Then the MC pressed play on the recorder, turned the volume up and out came Poppalocka's voice:

"You see young blood, the last time I was on the street mufuckas was dancing to another beat. Either they was pop-locking or break dancing, hoe hoppin or romancing. Pimpin, macking or playing, no matter which way it went or which way it go one thing for certain and two things foe sho' - you gotta stay pimpin even if you ain't got a hoe, cause without hoe you still gotta situation, so pimp yo way through yo situation and with that being said only thing left for me to say is congratulations and keep it pimpin, pimpin!"

"Like I said before, from the inside reaching out word from a certified seasoned vet in the game. Now without any more delays I bring to you all the Pimp of The Year, cuz this nigga been pimpin hard, I welcome to the stage Pimpin Stacks! The new Pimp King himself!"

Applause shot out from the crowd. When Stacks stood up all his hoes stood to attention and remained standing until he took the stage and waved his hand for everyone to be seated.

"Thank you, thank you! I must say that unlike the sucka that's born every day a pimp is born every so often. Being a pimp is to be able to lead a mufucka from self-destruction. For years growing up I thought that women had piss for brains. My father once told me: 'Boy, don't believe nothing a woman say, cause she got piss for brains!' So when my daddy divorced my momma I told her that she needed not to worry, because I was going to let her use my brain. She asked me why would she would need to use my brain; that's when I told her, 'cuz you a woman and women got piss for brains.' She smacked me all the way back into yesterday!

"A week later my aunt Queen came over and that's when I realized it's not that they got piss for brains, it's that the mufuckas ain't got no brains at all. My aunt gave me the game of life, she the only woman that I know on the planet to have two husbands, a boyfriend with a nigga on the side, and a nigga down the street she was fuckin, just because she wanted to fuck em," he explained.

"Now doing all that don't make a bitch no hoe, Queen had five kids, but took care of way more than that. What Queen did was pimpin! She was a pimpstress! And still is to this day. All my life I thought she knew voodoo and it wasn't until Big Pimpin Poppa-locka taught me 'you get more out of a bitch by keepin yo dick dry, then keepin it wet.' So apparently Queen wasn't fucking all them niggas, she was teasing all those niggas. She was a dick-teasing-ass-chick who controlled the mindset of a nigga with the T.D. syndrome. So here's to all the pimps, playas, hustlas, hoes, and tender duck mufuckas because without them a hoe wouldn't have a trick to turn."

Then Stacks raised his goblet in one hand and his cane in the other, with his crown on his head and shouted:

"Pimp pimp hoe-ray! Once again it's a muthafuckin hoe-lee-day!"

Tequila, Stacks' mainline hoe, felt something wasn't right. She looked around and noticed that next to each of Sergio's henchman stood a funny dressed pimp with a long overcoat and before she realized what was going on the fake pimps opened up their jackets and pulled out 9mm Uzis and started letting off on the guards.

She yelled, "STACKS GET DOWN!!" Then everywhere you turned bodies was droppin. LA, Shakim, Danz and Dem-Killers started poppin off.

'BOOM! BOOM! BOOM!'

Stacks looked around and behind him. He saw Sergio laying there in a puddle of blood, choking on his very own blood with his life leaving him with every breath. He was fighting to breathe. Stacks pulled out his twin Desert Eagle semi-automatic pistols and started returning fire. Bullets was flyin everywhere.

With precision he hit about five mufuckas back to back. All his hoes raced to the exit door while LA made his way over to Stacks, letting off round after round. His bitch Brooklyn came from under her chinchilla, with two 380s and yelled for LA to bring Stacks on out the door while she covered them. Then she went boldly moving in the direction that the shooters were, while letting off saying, "ROCKA BYE BABY!"

But the rapid fire of bullets left Brooklyn lying dead in front of the stage along with Megan and Summer. As Stacks, LA and Shakim with Dem-Killers made the way from the backyard to the front of the mansion shooting the way through with every step. Precious had pulled one of the limo trucks to the bottom of the stairs for Stacks. K pulled another one up, then Shakim and the rest of LA goons pulled the rest up while everybody jumped in the truck. Then they zoomed off screeching the wheels.

CHAPTER 2

Crunchy-Black

Stacks was seated at the head of the table as he thought back on the day's events that ended in a blood bath.

"Can somebody tell me what all that was about? Do any of ya'll know anything?!" he asked.

Precious was on the phone gathering information. One thing Stacks knew is that if his aunt Queen didn't teach Precious nothing, she taught her how to be street savvy. Precious was sweet as a sugar cane stick until you got her mad, then she was a cold hearted cunning stone cold killing ass bitch. Before she got into the strip club business she was a hired hit woman, whose body count was way into the hundreds. She was taught by the best, her father. He was a general in some hardcore black power movement from back in the 60's that had died out through the ages of time. But every now and then Precious would take on the contracts from underground mobsters. Only Stacks knew the things she did.

Precious hung up the phone and said, "My street connect said something about some nigga Crunchy-Black just paid off a group of young killers to take you out."

"Precious, who the fuck is Crunchy-Black and what's his beef with me?" Stacks asked.

"Man Stacks how the fuck am I supposed to know who the fuck he is? He probably got beef about one of them hoes you got in the other room," she replied.

"LA go tell them funky ass hoes I said get the fuck in here."

LA made his way to the door and opened it and holla'd for Stacks' hoes to come in.

"Which one of ya'll bitches know or even heard of a nigga named Crunchy-Black?" LA asked.

Silence fell over the room, that's when Stacks phone rang. He immediately picked it up and that's when Kee's voice came through the phone, "Aye yo slim, that was a paid hit from some big time drug boy out of Dallas. He got it out for you because you had his brother Black-Murda knocked off out in Dallas. That's supposed to be his little brother. Now if you want me to, for a hundred thousand, I can make all yo problems go away," said Kees.

"Aye yo Bleed, I want his whole family wiped out. But no kids or women. And Imma shoot two hundred thousand at you for your troubles," replied Stacks.

"I got you Stacks, consider it a done deal. And by the way congratulations on your award, you looked supa fly up there tonight and you got some bad bitches with yo team. Stay up and keep it real slim!" Kees said.

CHAPTER 3

Set-Up! Angry Dyke Style

Sin stood on the other side of the door listening to K and Precious go at it verbally for about 30 minutes. Then she heard footsteps coming towards the door. So she turned and ran into the next bedroom and quickly, but silently, shut the door. As she heard K mumbling to himself, "This bitch is crazy if she think Imma stay around here while she play house with this little Asian bitch."

As he continued to walk out of the front door he jumped in his car and speed off burning rubber.

Sin went into the room where Precious was laid across the bed crying with her head in her hands.

"Precious are you ok?" asked Sin.

"Yes! I'm fine," she sighed, while she took a deep breath. Then turned to Sin and said, "Sin baby I love you."

"I love you too Precious."

"I know you do Sin, but I love my man even more, he does things for me that no woman can ever do. His love for me is overwhelming and let the truth be told he says you are more of an expense than a contribution to our relationship," Precious explained.

"I can contribute. What is it that he wants? Because if its money I can go get all the money he needs!" replied Sin.

"No hunny, it's not money. He's not Stacks. K lives a simple life, he's not a pimp, hustler, or thug. All he is, is somebody who works for what he wants. If it wasn't for Stacks being his best friend and me being his girl, K would not be nowhere near the lifestyle he is living now. And after what happened at Stacks' event the other day he made a valid point. What if he would have lost me to a bullet to the head, chest, or main artery? Or if I would have lost him due to the same? K wants to get married and pay Stacks off, then sell our share in the club, as well as sell the club back in Ohio. Then he wants to move far away and live our life out together. Just the two of us. Me and him. Can you understand what I am trying to say Sin?" Precious asked.

"I understand, you're through with me? Like when I go on a date and they're through with me. My feelings don't mean nothing to you, they never did!" Sin said.

"No Sin, don't say that because, truthfully, I do love you and if K wasn't in the picture then you would be who I would be with day in and day out. No doubt. So don't never feel that way baby. But K is in the picture and he is who I'm going to be with and leave this crazy life behind. We can always be friends if you want me to. So that you don't have to go back to working for Stacks. I'll give you 25 percent in the club in Ohio. Then I'll sell the rest to an investor," said Precious.

"So when is all this supposed to take place?" asked Sin.

"Well, K said I have one week to decide and after that he is gone for good."

"Well then that gives me a week to come up with a decision as well…" Then Sin got up and walked out of the room, headed back to the space she occupied in the other room. She crawled into bed and contemplated how she was going to get rid of K, so that she could have Precious all to herself.

Later on that day Sin finally realized how she would do her devilish deed. She had contacted some Asian friends she had met while she had been in Vegas. She had hired them to kill one of the females in the club, then place the gun with the girl's cell phone under the front seat of K's car then place the body in the trunk of his car. So at about eleven o'clock that night K was doing his regular rounds with the girls. K noticed that one of the girls who was at work earlier, by the name of Sunshine, was no longer working the floor. So he called her cell phone once, then twice, back to back and no answer. Then K's phone rang as he was making his way to the office. He stumbled going up the stairs as he was trying to answer his phone. He was slightly intoxicated but he managed to do so.

"Hello K," said a female's voice on the other end. "Can you meet me in the parking lot garage? I need to talk to you about something away from the other girls. It's about some of the girls stealing money from you."

"Aight I'll be down there in a minute," replied K.

Once he had come to the garage he noticed that the lights in some parts of the garage were out. He paid it no mind as he called Sunshine's phone again. He heard it ringing so he followed the sound of Rick Ross' song 'Like a Bag of Money' being used as the girl's ringtone. The closer he got, he realized that the sound had to be coming from his drop top Lexus coup that sat off to the corner in the shadows of the darkness. So he kept letting the phone ring and started searching his car, reaching around on the floor in between the seats. Then when he reached under the seat, he felt the butt of a gun, he then thought to his self 'I could have sworn I left my gun at home.' So he grabbed the gun, gripping a good hold onto the handle pulling it from under the seat. It was a 9 mm with a silencer on the front. His phone rang.

"Hello?! Who is this?" asked K.

"Instead of worrying about me, you need to worry about what's in your trunk," a mysterious voice said. K went to the trunk with the gun still in his hand, opened it up then saw Sunshine shot straight though her head, right in between the eyes.

"Hello! What's the meaning of this?" K asked. "Why did you kill Sunshine?"

"I didn't kill her, you killed her. She's in your trunk and you are in possession of the murder weapon." Then the phone went dead.

K being the lame that he was when it came to crime, panicked, shut the trunk, threw the gun in the passenger side and jumped in the car and pulled off with the dead body in his trunk. Along with a murder weapon that now had his prints all over it. He called Precious who was too busy to answer, as she was getting her pussy sucked by Sin.

Fifteen minutes prior to K's mysterious phone call, the police had received a call telling them that a murder was committed and were given the description of K as being the murderer. So as K was pulling out of the strip club parking lot headed to get rid of the body, cop cars screeched to a complete stop all around making it impossible for K to escape. The cops were pointing shotguns, revolvers, and rifles at him, shouting to get out of his car with his hands up, turn off the ignition, and slowly step out of the vehicle.

"This is your last warning!" they said.

K shut the ignition off then opened the door as soon as he was outside of the car the police rushed him to the concrete and started putting handcuffs on him.

"Search the car!" one of the officers said. "Yes sir!" answered another.

While K was handcuffed face down on the ground one of the officers located the gun. Then another one popped the trunk and found the dead female. They picked K up and put him in the car after reading him his rights. Then rushed him to the police station where he was finger printed and booked for murder. K immediately called Stacks,

"Yo, what up?" asked Stacks.

"Aye yo Stacks this is K, I'm in jail for a murder I don't know anything about," explained K.

"You what nigga?" he replied, confused.

"Man you heard me Stacks. I said I'm in Vegas City Jail for a fucking murder I don't know nothing about. Somebody set me up and as of right now they are doing an excellent job."

"Where is my cousin? Why are you calling this phone instead of hers?" asked Stacks in an irritated tone.

"I couldn't tell you where she is Stacks. I mean ever since Sin has been around our relationship has been in the dumps. She is not answering her phone. That's why I called you," K said.

"Yeah K that's what's up, you my mans and I got you. Don't worry Imma have my son's mother to fly down there to get you out of this situation. So fall back," said Stacks. "How much is your bond?"

"As of this moment I don't have one," answered K.

"When you get one Imma wire the money to Kanisha."

"Who is Kanisha?" asked K.

"That's my lawyer, my baby momma. Like I said she's going to be there in the morning, trust me son! Right now Imma touch bases with Precious and have her come to see you so holla at you later K."

"Aight Stacks, good looking," replied K. As soon as he finished his phone call to Stacks he was escorted to a cell in the Homicide unit of the jail. K walked in, looked around the cell, turned to the officer, and complained about how badly the cell smelled. The Guard ignored him and turned around and walked off.

K was left in his cell with only his thoughts. He started to wonder to himself how he ended up in there. He was amazed at how fast his whole life had been turned upside down in a matter of hours. Everything happened so quickly. The guard returned and gave K a blanket with an apple and salami sandwich, then told K to get some rest because he was going to need it.

He was being charged with first degree murder. K grabbed the blanket then laid back thinking to himself that only if he would have never let Stacks talk him into selling weed and coke on campus to the upper class white crowd, that went to Syracuse with him, while he was in school for engineering.

'But once again instead of living my own life working at NASA I am suffering the consequences of living out Stacks' dreams,' K was thinking. He thought to himself about the time Stacks was smashing this shorty from the license bureau who hooked Stacks, Precious and his self, up with three "legitimate" fake I.D.s a piece, so that they could get paid ten thousand dollars for each time they got married to Indians from India, for US citizenship. But two days before the first three marriages were to take place, Stack's got busted fucking the girl's mother, so she cancelled the I.D.s out of the computer. Then everybody had to pay back the front money everybody had been paid by the Indian families.

Eventually K dozed off and went to sleep. Precious arrived two hours later at the police station, requesting to be able to see K. The officer told her she had to come back during regular visitation hours, since she was not an attorney. So Precious called Stacks to see how long it would be before the attorney would arrive. He explained that he just sent his private jet to pick her up and that she would be there first thing in the morning. After the conversation with Stacks, Precious left to go back to the house to collect her thoughts.

At the house Sin approached Precious acting like she knew nothing at all K's situation.

"Precious, are you ok sweetheart? You have a worried look on your face," said Sin.

"No, actually I'm not ok. I am highly upset because my man is locked up for first degree murder and the police wouldn't let me see him or tell me anything in detail as to what happened. They just said he is being charged with first degree murder," Precious explained, sadly.

"Wow, K don't seem like the type that would be a murderer, but you never can tell these days," Sin said.

"Sin, I know my man, he is no more of a murderer than Malcom X was a Christian," said Precious.

"Malcom who did you say?" asked Sin.

"Oh don't worry, you don't know who I'm talking about, just know K didn't kill nobody and when I find out who is behind all of this they will have to deal with me!" Precious said.

"Well Precious my love, I'm here for you. If you need anything. Are you hungry or thirsty?" Sin asked Precious, trying to hide her excitement.

"Nah Sin baby, just come lay with me so I can hold you while I go to sleep."

"KayShawn Malik! Your attorney is here to see you so stand up and turn around to get cuffed up!" mouthed the officer.

K jumped up off the concreate slab he was laying on. He had been awake since breakfast that was served at six in the morning. It was now seven thirty. The officer escorted K to the room where the attorney visits took place.

"Can you please remove the handcuffs off of my client? Hello Mr. Malik, my name is Kanisha Love and I was hired to represent you," the attorney introduced herself. "What you need to know is that as of right now you're being charged with first degree murder. During your arraignment, which is in about 30 minutes. I will try to get you a bond which I know the judge will give you. It's just that it will probably be an outrageous amount, but Stacks has told me no matter how much they ask for I am to pay it and get you out of here," she explained.

"I didn't kill nobody, so tell em that I am innocent!" said K.

"Ok Mr. Malik!" she said.

"You just call me K, like everyone else."

"Ok K, I need you to explain to me what occurred the night of the murder between you and the female that was killed," said Ms. Love.

"Look lady, I didn't kill nobody and the only way I know Sunshine is through employment. She worked as a dancer at my strip club," explained K.

"Well then how did she end up in your trunk with the murder weapon in your car?" she asked.

"I don't know! But what I do know is that about eleven o'clock last night I was doing my rounds and Sonya a.k.a. Sunshine, was not nowhere to be found. So I asked around and couldn't no one tell me where she was. Then my phone rang and I noticed that it was Sonya's cell phone," K explained.

"I answered it and a female voice asked me to come to the garage because she needed to let me know something without the other girls knowing. I assumed that she wanted tell me about one of the other girls stealing or something, so I went to the garage to meet her. But she was nowhere in sight. That's when I called her phone, but she never answered. I heard Rick Ross' song 'Bag of Money' playing, so I followed the sound which was coming out of my car. I reached in looking for the phone but instead I ended up finding a gun. Then my phone rang, I answered it and a female on the other end told me to look in my trunk and there she was, Sonya Wedge, dead as a door knob. After that I knew somebody was setting me up, so I was trying to get rid of the body and gun," K said.

"So there you have it, the whole truth and nothing but the truth."

"Aight my friend, what we have here is a major problem. But don't worry I am THE BEST when it comes to winning cases," replied Ms. Love.

"Alright Ms. Love, it is time for his arraignment hearing. Let's go Mr. Malik!" ordered the guard.

CHAPTER 4

Back in "H-Town"

"Pimpin Stacks is my name and pimpin hoes is my game. Imma P.I.M.P., a person intellectually manipulating pussy you see. I tell a hoe not to be a hater, be a motivator, participator, or better yet a congratulator. If a bitch ain't down with this pimpin, then I see that hoe later. I don't make hoes, I just break hoes. From my head to my toes, I stay ready to be chose, when I strike a pose foe them hoes, because I remain in some fly ass clothes. I take an amateur and turn her into a certified pro!" Stacks was rambling off at the mouth, drunk off of two bottles of Louie XIII and a fat blunt of some Hawaiian Blue Berry Kush.

He was out at the hottest strip club in Houston, Texas with a few pimp buddies of his, celebrating his Pimp King title, since shit went haywire a week ago at the Playaz Ball. Earlier that day the DC killer Quies called him and told him that he had to no longer worry about that crew in Dallas, they were now all pushin' up daisies.

"You see pimpin! The Playaz Ball is like the Olympics of pimpin, many pimps will make it, but only one pimp gone take it! *(The crown that is)*. You see pimpin, I won because of my cross country pimpin I do. From Syracuse to Kalamazoo. I was pimpin like a cross country fitness trainer… that's what I do!"

Stacks had on an apricot Giorgio Armani suit with a matching brim wearing the same color big block gators. Then this naturally curly haired red bone in a blood red Prada dress, showing off her flawless four feet nine frame, wearing a pair of Ostrich six inch stilettos that matched her handbag, walked straight up to Stacks and said:

"Hi, my name is Mercedes. I just moved here from a small town in Pennsylvania called White Oak. I am a student at TSU and I overheard you saying something about pimpin. I was wondering if I could have a word with you in private. If you don't mind."

"That all depends on you lil mama," replied Stacks.

"And how is that?" asked Mercedes.

"If it don't make dollars, then it don't make cents and if it don't make cents it can never make dollars. I'm all about a dollar, so my time is money and it cost money for my time. Now how much you willing to pay for mine?" he asked.

"Well how much is how much?"

"Well for starters you can start digging into your pretty little handbag of yours and break yourself off however much money you got in that mutha fucka, then that'll buy you enough time for me to decide how much more time I am willing to allow you to have," Stacks replied.

So she went into her Prada bag and pulled out three hundred and sixteen dollars, she tried to hand it to Stacks but he told her to put the money on the table over in the corner and wait till he got over there because a hoe ain't never supposed to put money in a pimp hand. No matter if she fresh off the track or if she fresh out the shower from cleaning her crack! Mercedes turned around and did as she was told. Fifteen minutes later Stacks showed up to show out no doubt, with a fresh bottle of Louie XIII with two glasses. He sat the bottle and glasses on the table, then slid onto the couch beside her and told her to pour him a drink as well as one for herself.

"Pimpin Stacks my name and pimpin hoes my game, what's your claim to fame? Are you trying to hoe down in the game?" replied Stacks.

"Excuse me? What did you say? Because I didn't understand one word of that terminology. I am only twenty-three years old and I was raised in a totally all white neighborhood. My mother is white and my father was a black pimp from San Diego named Cooty Loo. He was killed by one of his whores," she replied.

"So what you tellin me is that you fresh meat?" Stacks said.

"Whatever fresh meat is, as long as it's a good thing, then yes, I am fresh meat as you say. What I wanted to talk about is that I have been here for four days and school starts in another week and I have been looking for an honest 9 to 5, but with this budget cut and the country going through a depression I am having a hard time finding one," Mercedes explained. "My mother told me that a real pimp is one who takes care of his whores and I never sold pussy before or sucked a dick for money. But I had a boyfriend back home who I was with sexually about five times before I came out here. Up until about six months ago I was still a virgin. I lost my virginity to him so I wouldn't be a virgin in college."

"I tell you what, Imma help you save some money by moving you into my Estate and help you out with your problem, because a mufucka will stop paying bills before they stop buying pussy thrills," said Stacks.

"To be truthful Stacks, I was hoping that I could be your personal whore and that way I can take care of you and you can take care of me. I really don't wanna sell pussy to just anybody. I wouldn't know how to sell pussy," replied Mercedes.

"Well that's one thing I don't do, is run a rest haven for hoes, so get that out your pretty little head. The only way you gone be my hoe is if you earn yo keep. Now I'll start you off slow and let you work your way up to the top. I might have something for you to do to start making ends meet. First, what we need to do is get up out of here and head over to my spot."

Stacks got up and Mercedes followed. He grabbed his bottle of Louie and walked straight out the door. LA was waiting outside along with two of Stacks' body guards. Stacks got in the limo truck and headed home with his new addition to his Stable.

When Stacks arrived at the Estate, Winter had her bags packed leaving out the door as he was coming in. The other driver was loading her bags into a different limo.

"Hey Stacks daddy, I'm glad you made it home before I left. I am flying to Paris with Garvin. He has a medical client that wants some work done on her face and he requested my service. As soon as we land I'll wire no less than ten thousand. He's paying me twenty for the whole trip," she explained. "So whatever he give me it'll be wired to the account daddy. Now who is this little lady?"

"Oh this here is Mercedes. When you get back I want you to teach her a few tricks," said Stacks.

"Aight daddy, I gotta go. Oh yeah, Weezy, Pussy Cat, Shay, and Tequila all are on a plane to the Bahamas for a wedding. They were hired to do some ballin ass nigga out of San Antonio's bachelor party. They'll be back by Monday night. We tried calling but as I see, you were very busy playing daddy," Winter said.

"Bitch, in a minute. Imma be playin the pimp that knocked a bitch the fuck out if you don't get the fuck up out my face and get my money!" Stacks yelled.

"Yes daddy! Whatever you say, I didn't mean to get you upset," Winter apologized.

Then Stacks went into the house and saw Carmela looking in the refrigerator. She had on a tank top and pair of fishnet stockings underneath her boy short panties.

"What the fuck is you doing at home with everybody else out getting money?" asked Stacks.

"Stacks daddy, I'm making money in the basement on Skype. I came up to get me some whipped cream and a cucumber, so I can finish breaking this truck driver I got online paying by the hour," Carmela explained with a smirk on her face. "Actually I have a split screen goin on, this school teacher just paid up with his credit card for two hours."

"Oh Stacks can I go with her, please?!" asked Mercedes.

"That's on Carmela, but it's no time for a learning experience on live internet. She needs a seasoned hoe not no turn out," he said.

"Stacks baby, I said I was a virgin up until six months ago… to some dick. But I been suckin pussy since the 8th

grade and there is not a woman on this planet I can't please!" said Mercedes.

"Girl let's go be girls and let me see how good your tongue game is, because they call me Machine Gun Melly," Carmela said as the girls laughed. They disappeared into the basement and Stacks went upstairs and called Akelia in Ohio.

"Hello, Hello!" said Akelia. "Who is this? I can barely hear you. I'm at work up at the Vanity Wash so whoever this is just come up here. I'll be here until closing." Akelia hung up the phone and Stacks crawled into bed fully dressed, gone off that Louie XIII.

The next day Stacks woke at 12:30 in the afternoon with a headache. He got up and noticed that he was in his boxers and his outfit from the other day was hanging up on the back of the closet door, he immediately knew that Carmela had to undress him last night after he passed out. He made his way to the bathroom and once inside he turned on his security TVs that showed every room in the house. He saw Carmela in the fitness room, with Mercedes on the treadmill next to her. So he spoke to Carmela over the intercom,

"A yo Melly! I'm upstairs in my room about to get in the hot tub. I want you to fix me a cup of coffee and a t-bone steak with some scrambled eggs, then you and Mercedes come get naked in the hot tub wit me. I need to discuss a few things with the both of ya!"

Ten minutes later Mercedes climbed into the hot tub. Carmela put the tray of food and coffee on to connectors the hot tub had for food trays. Then she climbed into the tub with Stacks and Mercedes.

"So Carmela, how was she last night?" asked Stacks.

"Oh Stacks, she has a very passionate tongue, I think she will go far with your guidance and management," she replied.

"Ok! This is what I'm going to do with the both of ya'll. I have some new ideas that will generate some more money. What I want you to do Mercedes is, that after this session, have one of the drivers go to your dorm and bring back all of your belongings. Then you and Carmela go to the mall and pick out some sexy undergarments. I am going to have the photographer here when ya'll get back set up and ready to fuck up."

Stacks went on explaining his new plan, "I am going to turn the photos into poker cards and each one of you will have your own calendar and one with the both of you together. Imma call Jennifer and have her get in touch with all the major cell phone companies, to provide sexy wallpapers with voice recorded ring tones. Now in the meantime give me a reenactment of last night so I can see with my own two eyes, while I enjoy this brunch."

So both Mercedes and Carmela exited the hot tub and took to the floor and pleased one another while Stacks looked on!

Later on that day Stacks called Jennifer.

"Hello Jennifer," Stacks said.

"Yes Stacks, hello how are you?" she replied.

"How much longer are you going to be in India?" he asked.

"Probably for another week or two. What's wrong? Is everything ok?" Jen asked.

"Yeah, it's all good. I just need you to handle a few things for me in the states."

"Well fax me over all the information then I'll handle everything while I'm here," she said.

"Aight I'll do that. How is Cream? Tell her that I said my pockets feel light and to step her game up."

"Ok Stacks, will do exactly what you say. Is there anything else I need to do for you?"

"Nah, just wrap shit up over there and get back here. Until then, be easy - but not cheap!" laughed Stacks.

"Alright Stacks daddy, bye bye now," Jennifer said as she hung up the phone.

Then Stacks called Precious to see what's up with K's trial. She picked up on the second ring.

"Aye yo Precious, what's up?"

"I'm good, where you at?" she asked.

"Just chillin at the crib right now. So what they say about K?" asked Stacks.

"They denied his bond because they said that the gun that they found in his car was the same gun that killed two other females that are also strippers. So they said he is too dangerous for the streets. But I know K didn't kill no one, let alone three females," said Precious.

"Man that's fucked up! I don't know what to say except that I hope he's innocent and that Kanisha can help em out of this shit," replied Stacks.

"That's not the only thing that's bothering me," said Precious. "Stacks, I'm pregnant. With twins."

"How do you know its twins you're having? Is it not too early? I mean how many months are you?"

"I am three and a half months. I didn't say anything because I didn't know if I was going to have an abortion or not. But with K being locked up, the babies inside of me keeps me close to him. I don't know how to tell him," she said with sadness in her voice. "I should have said something before all of this took place."

"Look P, whatever happens I will be there for you. But let's change the subject for a minute, because all this emotional shit is not healthy for a pimp!" he said.

"Well, what you wanna talk about then Stacks?" Precious asked.

"Well for starters, I got fresh meat to promote. I knocked her off last night when I was out at the club. She's so green you could put the hoe on a golf course and she'll blend right in like a chameleon."

"So what you gone do with the girl if she that green? That mean somebody gots to show her the ropes and which one of them hoes you gone trust to do that?" Precious asked.

"You know what, you right. Imma put the hoe down my damn self. OH YEAH! I was thinking about putting together a pimp council and I gotta idea for Vegas, since G Tina shut down the Doll House behind the legal problems. So you know me, I'm always tryin to increase a dollar because making dollars ain't no problem," Stacks explained.

"Well Stacks Imma be honest, when, and if my baby get out of this bullshit he's mixed up in, then we're going to get out. While we still young. So I hope you can understand how I feel," Precious said.

"Oh come on P, you mean to tell me that a little bump in the road is big enough to make you change course?" he asked.

"Stacks, K is facing murder charges on three different counts. What's little about that bump? It's more like a fucking sink hole if you ask me!" Precious said with anger in her voice.

"That's yo problem. I didn't ask you shit. But if you tired of getting money and now all you thinking about is the dick; maybe I need to start pimping niggas for bitches like you, because this ain't the Precious I know. The Precious I know is a ride or die bitch who would be tryin to mentally and physically fuck the prosecutor, the Judge, or anybody else she may need to, so that she can get what the fuck she want. Then if that shit don't work, she would be putting niggas down for the permanent count to make shit go her way!"

"Well Stacks people change, I'm never tired of getting money. When we were younger all we talked about was making a million dollars and what we would do with that million dollars. And well I got at least two million and I know if I got two mill, then you definitely have multi-millions. What else can I ask for but a husband to be there for his kids, our kids," she said, trying to explain why she felt the way she did.

"It's Gucci baby, if you thru then I guess you thru. As for me I'm tryin be a billionaire before I get out the game. But I ain't mad at you, keep me posted on K and his situation. If ya'll need me for anything, then just know I am here for you, always. Aight P, I holla at you.."

"Ok Stacks, love you big cuz," Precious said as she hung up the phone.

The following morning Stacks woke up sweating profusely from a nightmare he had of him being arrested and going broke. So Stacks went into his walk-in closet, removed his dummy safe out the way and pulled the rug back. He punched in the code, 11-27-19-70, then a secret door popped open that lead to another walk-in closet.

In this room was a six foot safe with over five million dollars in cash, two million in diamonds, three hundred thousand in gold and a ready to go bag with a passport under an alias name, as well as one raw uncut diamond that was another five million.

He decided to get in touch with his brother, Ishan, who was a hard working nine to five, a full time husband and father that didn't wanna have nothing to do with Stacks. The only thing that bonded them together was the fact that they were blood brothers.

Ishan loved his younger brother Stacks, but didn't approve of his lifestyle or choices. Ishan was also a dedicated Muslim in the religion of Al-Islaam. Stacks took out the ready-to-go bag and one hundred thousand dollars cash to fly to his brother to keep away for him. The money was for the girls to go shopping. It had been awhile since he had treated them to something nice.

CHAPTER 5

The "Turn Out"

"Mercedes all you gotta do is go to room 333, knock on the door and when the old man opens the door, hit em with a smile and walk in like a pro. Then just follow his lead, he is paid up for a full hour or if he bust a nut before the hour up, then he is through," Stacks said.

"But Stacks, I am never going to be able to respect myself if I do this," Mercedes whined.

"Look Mercedes, I told you that the only way that you're going to be able to pay for your tuition is if you handle your business. Now if you don't think you are ready to be in my Stable, then get yo shit and go on with your life because I'm not into forcing a bitch to do anything. I got way too many hoes to be worried about one, especially one that is not tryin to live the lifestyle of the rich and famous. So what's it gone be?" Stacks asked.

"Livin' the life of a top notch bitch or the life of a dumbass college chick getting tossed up for free on campus, fucking and sucking everybody's dick? It's your choice, but I need to know cause I got a paid up client waiting on some pussy. So either you gone do it or Imma have one of my other hoes do it," Stacks said irritated.

"Aight Stacks, I'll do it, I'm just nervous being this is my first time," Mercedes said.

"Don't worry baby, I'll be right here checking the clock and remember use protection and put this in your purse." Stacks handed her a box cutter and sent her on her way.

Forty five minutes later Mercedes was back in the room where Stacks was posted up.

"Stacks, I feel nasty. I need to take a shower," said Mercedes.

"Come on we gotta go, ain't no time to take a shower. You shoulda done that before you came back down here," Stacks said shaking his head.

"Right now we gotta head to the Red Roof Inn on Airport Boulevard, out by Hobbie Airport. I got you two dates set up. They asked for Pussy Cat but since she is out of town, I need you to get that money for me," Stacks explained.

"The first guy is in room 113. He wants an hour, so soon as you go in get the money up front. He is a regular and he only usually lasts about 15 minutes, 20 minutes tops. Pussy Cat said he cum quick when she suck his dick and play wit his left nipple. So try that technique and if that don't work, it's up to you how quick he cum and when you finish wit him, the other guy is in room 415. He is another regular for Pussy Cat. the only thing is that he pays double for two. It's him and his wife, he likes to watch ya'll, then join in while you getting down with his wife. So once again, money up front, two thousand at five hundred a piece, for two hours…"

As Stacks drove up Airport Boulevard, Mercedes sat next to him with her arms crossed, with a mean look on her face. Stacks turned to her and said, "Look Mercedes, you a grown ass woman. You don't have to do none of this shit and I'm not gone keep repeating myself like a broken record. As a matter of fact, look. There you go, a help wanted sign for a waitress at the restaurant. Imma just drop you off over there and I'll have one of my drivers drop yo shit off back at the dorms on campus."

"No Stacks! Please don't do that, I don't wanna work as no waitress. I'm ok. I promise," she said.

"Aight then look like you mean it." Stacks pulled into the parking lot at the hotel and continued, "Take this phone and call me when you done. Then I'll let you know what room to go to after you finish wit them. Imma get you a room and leave the door unlocked for you. That way you can shower and be ready for what comes next. Now beat yo feet and let it do what it do baby. Remember, money first!"

"Ok Stacks," Mercedes mumbled as she got out the car and walked to her date's room, 113.

Five hours later Mercedes called Stacks and told him she was finished. He told her to meet him out front in an hour and that he got room 311 for her to take care of her business. Later on he was taking her to the track on Telephone Road. He had a room at The Mustang Inn ready for her.

Stacks pulled into the Red Roof Inn parking lot, in his brand new pearl white Cadillac ATS with all white guts, wood grain steering wheel, and the brains was blown out with limo tinted windows. He had five TVs put in with an eight thousand dollar surround system sitting on 22 inch Polkers that he bought a week prior to the Playaz Ball. He had just got it out of the shop. The whole car had been equipped with all the latest technology. He even had the "Lac" bullet proofed, including the tires. Mercedes came running out of the front entrance amazed at what she saw. He told her to get in the back seat and to put his money on the front seat,

"A yo Mercedes, I know you got all my money right? Because you two hours into your track time. So what's the math on the money you just put down?" he asked.

"Stacks, please don't sound so harsh, I got your money and the extra two hours came from the couple. So instead of two thousand they gave me four. They said that they wanna see me again, in about another week. I hope Pussy Cat won't be upset about that," Mercedes replied.

"Look, I'm the only shot caller when it comes to who do what and if that's what they want - that's what the fuck they gone get. So don't worry about the next bitches feelings cause the next bitch sho' don't give a fuck about yo young ass," he said.

"I was just thinking how I would feel if some other girl took money from me," she said.

"First off, don't none of the money belong to anybody but me, all money go one way, into a pimp's pocket and as far as you thinking don't do it no mo. Because you fucking up already, yo thinkin' gone get you some where you don't wanna be. Flat back to broke on campus. Looking and feeling like a dummy with all the time in the world to think. From now on do what the fuck I tell you and you'll be like gravy on a steak, real saucy baby."

Stacks then made his way to the track by The Mustang and drove around all the strips where the other hoes was strolling and gettin' money. Then he explained to her how to spot a cop and what to do to see if the person was a police officer, then he took her to her room, gave her the key with a bag full of condoms along with five dollars to pay for the pizza he ordered for her. She got out then went into her room to wait for the pizza while Stacks pulled off and headed to the crib.

He was having LA drive him to the airport. On the way there he gave strict instructions to swing by the strip and keep a close eye on Mercedes and to collect his money last on tonight from her. He wouldn't be back until the morning, due to the fact that he was going to Detroit to hook up with Big

Moe at the Casino to do some gambling. They arrived at the airport and Stacks had his private pilot to fly him to Detroit.

CHAPTER 6

High Roller

Stacks and Big Moe crossed the threshold of the Greek Town Casino. As soon as they entered the Casino, one of the pit bosses, who was a close friend to Big Moe, approached them and asked them if there were any special accommodations that needed to be met. Stacks requested a personal black jack table, because he would be playing a million dollars a hand or better. So the pit boss escorted Stacks and his friend to a table that still had the cloth on it. He removed the cloth and signaled for a dealer to come and open up the table. Moe told Stacks that he was headed to the dice table to try and get some money back because he had lost big a few nights ago. He stepped off, while Stacks took a seat and called Shakim, who he had flown in to meet him for this trip.

"Aye yo Sha, I'm ready! Everything is set up, bring in the money."

"Aight son, I'm on my way, which table you at?" asked Shakim.

"As soon as you step in come to the black jack tables and you'll see me posted up," he replied. Shakim came walking in with two brief cases that had over five million dollars in them. Then gave them to Stacks. Then Stacks handed the money to the pit boss and asked for the chips. Ten minutes later he came back to the table with five and half million dollars' worth of chips. Stacks signaled a waitress over to his table, he ordered a double shot of One Five One, his favorite drink to have while gambling big. Then he pushed two million in chips across the table to his dealer.

"Scared money don't make no money and ain't no money like hoe money, cause hoe money is blow money!" Stacks said with a smirk.

The dealer looked at Stacks for a moment then dealt Stacks a Queen. The waitress returned with his double shot, he took it to the head, then told her to keep em coming. He turned to the dealer who was showing a Ten. Then the dealer dealt Stacks an Ace of Hearts. The dealer flipped over a nine which gave him the total of nineteen - he then flipped over a three. Stacks won the first hand, then shouted:

"BITCHES AND HOES EVERYTHING GOES! LADY LUCK IS MY MUTHAFUCKIN HOE!!"

Stacks kept the four million on the table and told the dealer to deal em. The dealer dealt Stacks an Ace of Spades the first round and dealt himself a six of Clubs, the second round Stacks got an Ace of Diamonds.

Stacks set up a second pile worth four million then said:

"Split em cause pimpin ain't dead and the hoes ain't scared. Lady Luck gettin fucked tonight and bringing this pimp back all the bread!" Stacks exclaimed.

The dealer's hand was showing a six and an eight, then he drew a ten to bust. Stacks won again! Now he had sixteen million on the table. The pit boss reappeared, tapped the dealer on the shoulder and told him to go take a break. He told Stacks that the table he was now sitting at was shutting down and that there was another table with one other gentleman that had been gambling a million dollars a hand as well and if he cared to join him.

Stacks looked at the table where the pit boss had pointed to and noticed that the man sitting there happened to be the Russian that he sold Mandy to last time he was at the Greek Town Casino. Stacks sat there for a moment, then his waitress handed him another double shot of One Five One, as he took the drink he handed her a one hundred dollar chip as a tip and told her he was moving to another table. He pointed to the table, she nodded and went on to tend to other customers. Stacks got up and told Shakim to carry his money and chips to the other table.

He sat down and observed the game that was already taking place. He looked up at the Russian and noticed that he had a mysterious look on his face, then the Russian asked, "Are you here to gamble or are you going to sit there and stare at me like you don't know who I am?"

"I don't Gorilla Pimp and I don't Gorilla bet, because to me a Gorilla is a branded mufucka and its obvious that Lady Luck separated herself from me as soon as I sat down at this table," Stacks replied.

Stacks stood up and told Shakim to cash in his chips and that they were getting the fuck outta there.

"Signs and symbols are for the conscious mind and a pimp like me know when to fall back and play the cut like a band aid."

Then his phone started to vibrate. He looked down at the number and saw that it was Winter. He answered it as he was making his way out the door.

"Yeah what's up Winter?" Stacks asked.

"Stacks we are all back at the Estate, when are you coming back home? We miss you daddy!" replied Winter.

Stacks replied, "I'll be back in the morning and when I get back we will hold a meeting, so let everybody know I said if they're going on a date to schedule them all for after the meeting."

"Ok Stacks, I will see you when you get here," She replied.

"Aight later."

As soon as he got off the phone, the Russian came walking up.

"Hello my friend," he said.

"I don't know you like that so keep the word 'friend' out of yo vocabulary when you referring to me. But what's on your mind?" Stacks replied.

"It seems as if you are upset about something. May I ask what it is that has you on edge?" asked the Russian man.

"I'm not on edge, I just don't like being questioned by the police about the next man's doings. Especially when it does not involve me," he said with irritation in his voice.

"Are you referring to the female we did business over? I think her name was Mandy, if I'm not mistaken."

"You know damn well who I am talking about. If you was going to kill that hoe why not have just killed her without paying me. You could have kept me the fuck out of it and handled your business," Stacks replied.

"I am a business man just like you are. You see, you sell women who do sexual acts for money who bring the money back to you. Whereas for me, I sell women to a secret group of people who want to remain anonymous, for their over aggressive sexual activities, and their cruel and unusual fantasies. So I invest in my business by buying women from pimps or hired kidnappers; who kidnap only women who are either prostitutes, drug addicts, or women who are destined for a life time prison term and sell them to my clients who then torture them during sex; or who want to actually just pay to live out a fantasy of killing a woman," the Russian man explained, "Kind of like that movie, Hostel 1 and 2. You know, the one I'm talking about right?"

"Yo! You is a sick muthafucka, you and your damn clients. You don't have to worry about me or any of my hoes and from now on, you tell your kidnappers that if they come across a prostitute with a money symbol on the back of their neck to leave em alone, because she is one of my many hoes that are part of my establishment. AIGHT?! Cause if any of my hoes go missing, I'll be seeing you personally," then Stacks turned around and walked out of the door with Shakim right on his heels. As they headed to the limo Stacks had waiting out front to take him to the airport to fly back to Houston, Stacks called Big Moe.

"Aye yo Moe, I'm headed back to the Honey Comb hide out. I'll get at you later."

"Aight Stacks holla at me when you get back into town, I wanted you to go check the spot out and look at the job we did on the carpet for you. But I get at you, stay safe bro!" Moe replied.

"Yeah, no doubt, peace!"

CHAPTER 7

Dope Fiend

All of Stacks hoes were seated in their assigned seats at the large meeting table. Stacks stood up, then popped open a bottle of Don Perrie Aun. He poured himself a nice portion into his pimp cup. He then took his drink before he addressed his stable full of hoes,

"Today is a new day, a brand new beginning for everybody in this room. All of you have righteously earned their place at this table, as well as being able to continue to be a part of this establishment. So therefore it is time to raise the bar above and beyond anything average when it comes to my pimpin and your hoeing... In doing so I have asked a professional tattoo artist to come here in a few hours, so that each one of you can get a dollar symbol tatted on the back of your neck to express your loyalty."

Stacks continued, "Also to exemplify my pimpin, there is a new way to sell that pussy without even givin up the pussy. I'm not saying that you all are not still going to be flat back hoeing, so don't get it twisted. It's just that virtual reality is a new space age way for pimpin and hoein. I bought a building in the downtown for us to open a virtual sex shop. We will be selling everything from porn, sex toys, aphrodisiacs, to virtual sex in the many private rooms - all the way to flat back fucking in the basement. Also the All-Star game is here this weekend and whichever one of you make that pussy squirt the most cream, get a three day trip wit me on a Carnival boat ride to the Bahamas. Cause like Wu-Tang said 'Cash rules everything around me! Get the money! Dolla dolla bill ya'll!'" Stacks chuckled.

"Also I have hired a game designer to design a game for all electronic game devices. Each one of you will play a different character in the game. It'll be like Grand Theft Auto, but instead it will deal with pimpin' and hoein' on three different levels. Now let's close this meeting in the usual fashion. Stacks then held out the hand with his pinky ring on it while each hoe came up and kissed the ring as they exited the room. When it was Tequila's turn to kiss his ring, Stacks pulled his hand away and told her he was not though with her and for her to sit back down.

"Tequila are you still seeing that FBI client? If so, I need you to get him to look into K's case. I hear that the Feds picked it up due to the silencer and both the guns he had. Which was his gun and the murder weapon," said Stacks.

"Alright Stacks, I'll do that for you. Is that all you wanted?" replied Tequila.

"Yeah that's it for now."

Shay woke up with flue like symptoms and in intense pain. She got out of bed and tried to make her way to the bathroom. But instead she fell to the floor holding her stomach, trembling while sweat ran down her forehead. Weezy ran over to help Shay as she began to vomit all over herself and the floor.

"Girl, Stacks is going to get rid of yo ass if he ever find out that you back on drugs." It had been two weeks since Shay had snorted her first bag of heroin, relapsing from being drug free for all this time. She wasn't even making money like she use to before she had started using again. Weezy had been putting in over time to make extra money to give Stacks for Shay's weekly payments, while Shay laid up in hotel rooms slamming and snorting H.

"Please help me Weezy! Stacks can't find out. Oh God, Weezy I need a fix, please call Bobby for me, tell him to meet you wit a bundle," Shay pleaded.

Weezy stared at her friend laying in the middle of the floor surrounded by her own vomit clutching her cramping stomach.

Bobby was an OG shot caller for the Vice Lords. He had been in Houston after leaving Chicago in search of a new territory to sell his drugs. His "Smack" was so good that he had the whole South side of Houston on lock. Bobby was a heartless mufucka who was known for hooking some of the baddest bitches and hoes on drugs. His number one move was to trick wit a hoe or spend big money on a bitch then lace they weed wit heroin. By the time they figured something was wrong with their bodies they would already be hooked.

"Shay you know I don't fuck around wit that low life ass nigga. Especially since he the one who got you hooked back on drugs. I told you not to fuck wit dat nigga," Weezy said.

Shay buried her head in between her legs, feeling sick from not having any of her "get right" powder. Also feeling ashamed for allowing herself to get re-hooked on such a deadly drug, wishing she would have listened to Weezy about fucking wit that nigga Bobby.

It all started with Bobby picking her up on a late night, in his triple black BMW, with moccasin leather interior. He asked her if he could spend some money on her. So she took him to be a trick, but all along he was tricking her by him always picking her up and taking her to a room on the South side, drinking, and smoking weed.

He told her that he was on probation and couldn't smoke because he had to take weekly piss tests. But he was always good because that was his hustle. So she didn't think nothing of it when he only wanted her to suck his dick and blow smoke out her nose while doing it. It wasn't until she woke up dope sick one day, craving his weed, she told him that she wasn't feeling good and that she needed some of his European weed. He told her that she had to be sick from the heroin the weed was laced with. That's when she flipped out on him, then said "fuck it" and asked him if he would find her some H.

Bobby had told her that he just bought some to sell, since his weed connect got knocked. He sold her a bag a day, until her needs grew stronger and she started doing a bundle or two a day to keep that monkey from kicking her ass up and down the track.

"Please Weezy I won't ask you to do this again, just let me borrow some money so I can get right. That way I can go make my own money, plus enough to pay you back," Shay begged.

"What about the money to pay Stacks? You forgot about that hun? Damn Shay, dial his number."

Shay handed Weezy her phone after pressing one for speed dial. Shay then commenced to vomiting all over again.

Bobby picked up on the second ring, "What up Charlie?"

"Hello Bobby, it's Weezy."

"Oh you finally ready for me to take you out on a date?" Bobby asked.

"Not the way you treat women. I'll never date or trick wit you," she replied.

"Are you uptight about that fiend ass bitch Shay? She had that coming; it was always in her to be a dope fiend ass junky. But you, you're different. I could see a future wit you as one of my girls, doing big things. Shay is just another trick that got caught slipping." Bobby said.

"Anyway can I meet you at Denny's on Airport Boulevard? Shay is sick, you're the only person she know to get her medicine from. So I'll be there in fifteen minutes," Weezy said.

"Aight I'm on my way, but instead if you get there before me, wait in the gas station's parking lot. That's connected to Denny's lot," said Bobby.

Weezy got up and told Shay she'd be right back and to just hold on, it wouldn't be long. She then went to Stacks and told him she needed to take the Lambo so she could meet her date. He gave her a c-note told her to take the car through the wash and fill up the tank and to bring back the change with the other money she was going to make. Weezy thought to herself that she was going to have to call a regular and make some money, so Stacks wouldn't get suspicious. But she needed to hurry back for Shay to get right. Weezy pulled out of the Estate headed to Airport Boulevard to meet Bobby. As she pulled into the gas station she spotted Bobby sitting in his BMW with the top down. She pulled up next to him and went to hand him the money for the bundle…

"You keep that for yourself, cause Shay told me how your pimp make ya'll pay him a mandatory five thousand dollars a week," Bobby said.

"It's not like that. Stacks don't put his hands on none of us. We pay him because of the life he has given us. Also because he treat us better than any pimp has ever treated us," she replied.

"You need to come with me, so I can show you how good life can be without selling your body. That same five thousand a week you give him you can make for yourself, taking trips all around the United States as my mule. I don't usually pay, but twenty five hundred a week or you can sit in one of my many dope houses and make the same amount instead of getting pimped and taken advantage of. As for your girl Shay, she is nothing like you. She is TPT - Trailer Park Trash. You're more like a diamond in the mud. I'm just keeping it real," he said.

"Well I'll keep it real wit you. Front me a thousand dollars and I'll take you up on that trip this week. And you promise I don't have to sell no pussy, plus I get to keep all of the four thousand since I'm asking for a thousand now," Weezy suggested.

Bobby reached under his seat pulled out a brown paper bag and handed Weezy twenty five one hundred dollar bills,

"Now you'll get your other half when the trip is over. Take this phone and when I call be available to leave immediately. Ok?" Bobby replied.

"Thank you Bobby and please let this be between the two of us. I don't even want Shay to know." Weezy got out of the car and back into the Lambo and drove back to the Estate and went straight in to give Shay the heroin.

Shay was now in the bed sweating profusely. She sat up and opened the first pack and folded it then put it to her nostril, She sniffed real hard while leaning her head back. A few seconds later the pain she was feeling was gone. As she began to be overtaken by the smooth overwhelming high. She then got up out of the bed, walked over to the closet where she had a bag full of utensils to use so that she could enjoy the next bag in her veins. She grabbed the bag out of the closet, sat it on the dresser, and then pulled out a spoon, a needle with a syringe, and a small tube of water. She fixed everything up by pouring the heroin onto the spoon with a little water, sucked it up with the needle after she held the lighter under the spoon. She clinched the needle in between her teeth and tied a flexible rubber tube around her arm, found a good vein, and stuck the needle in her arm. She then shot the poison into her arm.

Weezy stood there looking in disgust as she thought about what Bobby had said about Shay being a dope fiend and how it was always in her. Shay laid back in the bed and went into a deep nod. Weezy walked out of the room and went into Stacks' office and sat the money Bobby gave her on his gold platter. Cheri, Pussy Cat and Carmela came walking into the office.

"How long is it going to be before you think Stacks gone find out about Shay getting high and you covering for her?" Cheri asked.

"I am only tryin to help her until she can get some help for herself," Weezy answered.

"If I was you I would let her be. She don't want no help and you know what the consequences are in life when you live life the way she is. As far as I'm concerned the bitch need to get the out before she fuck up, then Stacks start treating us all like shit because if one bad apple. So you can let her know, that I said she got 24 hours to check into a hospital or I'm letting him know," Pussy Cat said.

"I agree," said Cheri.

"Me too," Carmela chimed in.

CHAPTER 8

The Lock Up and Beat Down

The longer K sat in jail, the more upset he became about the helpless situation he was in. The judge denied his bond so now he had been put in the county jail with the other "hardcore" criminals. Precious was visiting him as she always did.

"K baby, when all this is over with we are moving out of the country to raise our kids in a much safer, better environment," Precious said.

"Precious who's to say that I will even get out of this?" he asked.

"Just think positive, I know you're going to overcome this and we will look back at this as another bump in the road." They sat there looking into each other's eyes, smiling, talking time away. Before they realized it, the guard was telling K that his time was up.

"Ok, Precious I'll see you tomorrow same time baby."

"I love you K, keep your head up and remember to stay positive."

Precious got up put her hand on the glass as K did the same. Precious blew a kiss then turned around and walked away.

Things were not going the way Sin had thought they would between her and Precious since K was out of the way and behind bars. Their sex life had dwindled down to nothing. They were not even talking as much. Precious stayed on the phone either with K or the lawyer every day. If she wasn't on the phone she was either writing love letters or going to visit him. Sin was starting to feel like everything she had done was in vain.

"Precious I was hoping that the both of us could go to a movie tonight. That new movie 'Call,' with Hallie Berry, comes out tonight I think," Sin suggested.

"I can't go to a movie while my man is locked up. Plus tonight is our anniversary. It's the day that we first made love to each other ten years ago," said Precious.

"I only thought that a movie would do some good, to help you stop stressing over K being gone," Sin replied.

"A movie will induce my loneliness because K always would hold my hand through the whole movie," Precious said with sadness.

"What about me? Am I not capable of holding your hand and making you feel good?" Sin replied.

"You must not ever been in love with a man before. It's nothing like the love of a man. I don't know how to explain it. Except for me saying it's like feeling no pain, being able to overcome all obstacles, having an eternal heart. True love of a man is that selfless love," Precious explained. "It's more powerful than lust. It conquers all doubt. You can feel it in every inch of your body. I mean every love will be tested, but the true love of a man detaches itself from failure, for it passes all tests in the end," Precious said passionately.

"If you love him that much, then why sleep with me and share intimate moments with me over and over?" Sin asked.

"Please Sin, don't make this any harder than it has to be. With you it's me being that other person. Living out my fantasy," Precious explained. "You see, most women don't want to admit that being sexually involved with another woman is their ultimate fantasy. So they cover it up by cheating on their man. Or if they are not in a relationship they hide it by sleeping around with many men. They might even go as far as getting two dicks at once," Precious said trying to get Sin to understand where she was coming from. She continued, "Whereas for me, I love what we have. I'm just not 'in love.' The only real time a woman falls 'in love' with another woman is when she has been hurt deeply and don't want to feel that same pain ever again. So they fall in love with another woman who is equally the same."

"I don't believe you. I know you're in love with me. You just don't want to admit it. The way you hold me, kiss me, and sex me, tells it all. You're just stuck on K because you have known him for a long time. That's why I did what I did to get him out of the way. So WE can be together and I hope and pray he rots in jail," Sin said, angrily.

"EXCUSE ME?" Precious said shocked by what had just came out of Sin's mouth.

"You heard me, I hate K," Sin said, as tears started rolling down her cheeks. "It's your fault he is in jail! Had you not made me feel as good and as wanted as you did, I would have never paid to have K set up the way I did. I love you Precious and will do anything to have you to myself!"

As Sin spoke those words Precious felt like a knife had been dug deep into her heart. She had never felt so betrayed in her life. Precious fought back her tears then the blood in her body rushed to her head. Then all hell broke loose! Precious swung a hay-maker, hitting Sin in the face and instantly breaking her nose, blood came rushing down from Sin's nose as Precious commenced to whooping Sin all over the room like Layla Ali did Joe Frazier's daughter.

This beating went on for about 20 minutes, before Sin got a boost of energy. She socked Precious in the face so hard

Precious stumbled back. Sin then kicked Precious dead center of her muffin, so hard it left Precious bent over long enough for Sin to make a run for the front door. Sin made it out of the door, running to the car that Precious had bought her; which was sitting at the end of the driveway. As soon as Sin put her hand on the car handle with one hand and using the other to put the keys in the door, Precious had snuck up behind her, then hit her in the back of her head with a baseball bat knocking her unconscious.

It was a hot sunny day and the whole neighborhood was outside, a guy who was jogging past was able to tackle Precious before she laid another deadly blow to Sin who was laying on the ground with blood gushing from the back of her head, from the blow of a baseball bat striking her and cracking her skull open. Precious was hysterical, as she tried to fight off the 200 pound man, begging him to let her go.

"Please get off of me so I can kill that bitch! She set my boyfriend up! Get the fuck off of me now muthafucka!" By the time Precious ran out of breath and somewhat calmed down, the ambulance had arrived giving immediate attention to Sin, who had lost way too much blood. The police were next on the scene asking questions. They arrested Precious and took her downtown for booking where she quickly phoned Stacks.

"I wonder who the fuck this is calling my phone from Las Vegas Police Department?" Stacks said after looking at his caller i.d. on his house phone. "Hello, who is this?"

"Stacks this is Precious."

"Why are you calling my land line and not my cell?" Stacks asked.

"I tried your cell and it went straight to voicemail, I've been arrested for aggravated assault," she explained.

"Who the fuck did you assault?"

"I beat the breaks off Sin, I lost it. I don't remember anything except that she told me that she is the one who set K up. She hired someone to kill that girl they found in K's trunk and planted the gun in his car, so he would go down for homicide. That way she and I could be together. She told me everything, that's when I spaced out on her," Precious said. "I need you to pull some strings and get me out of here!"

"Where is Sin at right now?" Stacks asked.

"She was rushed to the hospital."

"Aight P, I got you. I'm on my way to Vegas. Just chill out, I'll be there before the nightfall."

"Aight Big Cuzz, love you," Precious said as she hung up the phone.

Stacks hung up the phone, then called LA over the intercom in the guest house.

"Aye yo, LA get a few of the fellas together we're taking a trip to Vegas, I gotta see what's up with Precious...."

Stacks arrived in Vegas and went straight to the police station. Once there he requested to see Precious. They denied him and said she had a $1,500 bond, no ten percent. Stacks paid the bond and waited for Precious to be released. Thirty minutes later she was let out of the side door.

"Precious, over here!" Stacks shouted. Precious ran up to Stacks and gave him a bug with a kiss on the cheek.

"Thank you cuzz. Let's go find that bitch Sin so I can finish what I started," Precious said.

"Yo, chill the fuck out. Sin was released from the hospital an hour ago. I had LA go pick the bitch up, then take her to a hotel on the outskirts of town. I need to know what jumped off wit you two. That way I can know how to deal with this situation when I get to the hotel she's at," said Stacks.

"Like I said, we were involved in an emotional conversation about how I feel about K. When she was trying to get me to understand how deeply she felt about her and I being together. I told her that she basically was a fantasy being lived out. That's when she told me that she had K set up, so that he would not be in our way. She didn't go into detail about how she did it. That's because I choked her out," said Precious.

"Look! I want you to go to the house and relax until I get there. As of right now I'm going to go to the room to see what she has to say about all of this. I want to see how we can get K out of this crazy jam he in. Give Kanisha a call, she is still here somewhere in Vegas. I just wired her some money last night. Explain to her what's going on, then tell her I said for her to meet me at your house tonight!"

"Ok Stacks, PLEASE get that bitch to tell you everything," Precious pleaded.

"Fuck that bitch Precious!" said Sin. "I don't give a fuck if K get the death sentence. She should have never played with my emotions. Wouldn't none of this be happening if she would have kept it real with me from the beginning of our relationship. She had me thinking that she was in love with me the whole time," Sin said.

"Look bitch, watch how you come out your muthafucking mouth when you talking to me. Ain't nothing change with my pimpin, you still a hoe to me. Now what I wanna know is, who the fuck did you pay to set my mans up with them murder charges he facing? This is not about you or Precious' pussy bumping asses. This is about my homeboy K who is sitting in jail because of two emotional bitches. Now if you wanna love to get them fourteen staples out your head, then I suggest you provide me with what I need to know," Stacks said with annoyance.

"Stacks if I tell you that, then I'll still die because they will kill me," Sin replied.

"LA give this bitch a piece of paper and a pen," he ordered.

LA gave her the pen and paper he had got from the front desk.

"Now Sin what I want you to do is write exactly what you did onto this paper. You can leave out who you hired but I want you to explain why you did it and how much you paid the people to do it. Date it and sign it. That's the only way Imma let you live.

Now what the courts will do to you is probably give you a crime of passion charge. You'll do about five to seven years then be deported back to your country," Stacks said.

"What about my mother who is very sick? I send her money at least once every 90 days for her medicine. I rather die than to live and not be able to help my momma," Sin replied.

"You do this, then you got my word I'll see to it that your momma is taken good care of," Stacks reassured her.

"Ok Stacks, I trust you and I'll write it, hand me that pen…"

Sins finished writing the letter then Stacks told LA to stay with her while he went to Precious' house to meet Kanisha to discuss getting K out of jail immediately.

Once Stacks entered Precious' house, he approached Kanisha who was out back on the patio sippin on a martini.

"Good evening Kanisha," Stacks said as he made his way over to the outside bar to pour himself a drink. "How is everything going with you tonight? You're looking lovely to the naked eye."

"Cut the small talk Stacks, what is it you need from me?" she replied.

"Why are you so bitter and yet lookin so pimp-a-licious?" Stacks asked.

"Why so bitter and me looking pimp-a-whatever you said, you can save that talk for one of your many hoes. Remember I am the mother of your child and you have the audacity to walk up in here and act as if everything is ok between the two of us. The only reason I'm here is on a professional level, a hired attorney," said Kanisha.

"Hold on Kanisha, don't no bitch, hoe, or women speak to me out they cum catcher the way you just did, so come again, baby momma or not," Stacks said.

"I apologize Stacks it's just your son is six years old and he needs a father figure around in his life. He needs someone to teach him how to live life from a male point of view," Kanisha said.

"Aight, I tell you what - for his birthday I'll come get him. Now let's get down to business. What I have here is a written statement from that hoe Sin, stating that she hired someone to set K up, out of the love she has for Precious."

Precious came walking onto the patio, "Did I hear you say that she did it because she loves me? That bitch crazy?" Precious asked.

"Yeah! That bitch all screwed up behind you two fucking with each other. That hoe was a money getting ass bitch. Anyway, what's the plan in how we gone get K out of jail?" Stacks asked.

"First thing first, Sin must turn herself into the police. After that I'll make copies of the statement, take one to the district attorney's office, one to the judge and keep the original on file that way the D.A. and judge can sign off on an immediate release, which, within hours, after that K will be released. Now are you sure Sin won't say she was forced or threatened to write this statement?" Kanisha replied.

"Nah, she won't do that because I gave her my word not to kill her as well as send her sick mother money while she is serving her time," he said.

"Ok then, if that's all said and done let's finish the night off with a bottle of Louie XIII, then take care of everything that needs taken care of in the morning," Precious said.

Chapter 9

Consequences

Two days later Stacks was back in Houston, Texas at his Estate shooting a game of pool with Tequila while Winter, Cheri, and Pussy Cat took turns on the stripper pole he had installed. Sin had been arrested, K was released from jail, with all charges dropped, and the charges Precious had been facing were dropped, as well. Stacks paid off two C.O.s in the Vegas County Jail a hundred thousand a piece to kill Sin. It was all on the news that an 'Asian Murder For Hire Prostitute Hangs Herself In Her Cell.'

"Stacks there is something I need to let you know about Shay," Pussy Cat said.

"Shay? What about her, she left about an hour ago with Weezy to the track," Stacks said.

"Weezy might have went to go get money, but Shay back on that diesel, heavy. Weezy been carrying her for a while now. Shay get money but she spends it on dope from this Chicago nigga named Bobby," said Pussy Cat. Stacks threw his pool stick down then walked up to Pussy Cat.

"Are you talking about Vise-Lord Bobby? The same nigga who is running around here turning bitches out?" asked Stacks.

"Yes Stacks, that's the Bobby I'm talking about," she said.

"Cheri bring me my phone off the bar counter," Stacks ordered. He dialed Shay's phone, let it ring five times then it went to voicemail. He tried it again and the same thing happened. He then did the same thing with Weezy's phone and no answer. He walked over to the bar poured himself a drink, sat down, and flicked on the TV. Without saying anything he motioned for everybody to leave the room.

It was a hot, beautiful summer day when Mercedes walked into a Mexican bar, not too far from the Mustang. She was hoping to catch a date because it was too hot outside for her. She walked up to the bar and ordered herself a drink. A potential customer approached her from behind.

"I'll pay for that," a short, stubby Mexican man said to the bartender.

"Thank you mister," Mercedes said.

"Oh, it's nothing but money and there's plenty more where that came from. What's your name?" he asked.

"My name is Mercedes, What's yours?" she said, flirting.

"I'm Paylong and there is a good reason for me having that name. I never seen you around here. Are you new in the neighborhood?" answered Paylong.

"Yes, I am new to Texas all the way around. Are you from Texas?"

"No I have been living here for a few years now. I own a construction company. Are you looking for work?" he asked.

"Yes I am, just not the type of work you are offering. I'm looking to make some money from me doing what I do best…" Mercedes said.

"And what do you do best?"

"Please let's not play childish games. You and I both know what I'm talking about. I have a golden pussy with a platinum mouth, so are you willing to hire me for the job?" Mercedes asked.

"Yes, where can we go?" Paylong said anxiously. Mercedes stood up and said, "The Mustang, I have a room there." They both began to make their way to the door, headed for the Mustang.

Stacks had dropped Cheri off on a date and headed to the Mustang himself. As he was pulling in, the usual sensor bell with the irritating sound went off as it always did when someone went through the entrance. He pulled into a parking spot and noticed the Mexican exiting Mercedes room, with his face lit up like a Christmas tree. As soon as he got into his car and pulled off, Stacks got out of his truck and walked to the door of the room she was in.

'KNOCK, KNOCK, KNOCK.'

Mercedes looked through the peep hole. When she saw Stacks she opened the door. He walked in and the room smelled of bad pussy reeking in the air. It was so bad Stacks opened the door to let some fresh air in. Stacks noticed the blood spots on the sheets of the bed and open rubber packs with used condoms on the floor. She also had her school books in the corner by the table.

"What's up Mercedes? I see you getting your grind on."

"I'm not grinding, I'm working in between classes on campus. I've been taking the bus, it's a straight shot to down town," said Mercedes.

"Working where?" He asked.

"I'm talking about selling pussy. I like the word 'working' more than grinding. It sounds more professional. It helps me feel better doing what I do. Your money is in the bathroom ceiling. Let me get it for you."

She went to the bathroom and came back with eighty two hundred dollars, a week's worth of sucking and fucking. She put the money on the table, then told him how much it was. Stacks grabbed the money stuffed it into his True Religion jeans, then told her he'd be back in 20 minutes so she could shower real quick. He left real quick and drove to McDonalds to get her a fish combo with an orange soda. When he got back to the room, Mercedes was just getting out of the shower. Stacks handed her the food and told her to eat fast and get dressed. He opened the door and told her he would be waiting in his truck. He told her to have the maid clean her room because he didn't want her to run any dates in that filthiness.

Later that day...

Shay was down on her knees sucking the dick of a heavyset white guy who was a trucker. With one hand on his dick and the other picking bills out of his wallet, one by one and slipping them into her own pants pocket. She thought he hadn't noticed but after he came he grabbed Shay by her head and punched her dead in the eye. He stood up pulling his pants back on. Shay knew she was busted, then he started punching her in her face over and over saying, "you dumb bitch did you think that you could rob me and I wouldn't notice. I been messing around with you hookers for quite some time now!" He kept punching his fist into both of her eyes.

"I knew all along you was skinning my pockets. All you hookers do that! It's the greedy ones like you I don't like. Couldn't be happy with the first bill; you just had to keep on skinning - you greedy ass slut!"

Shay was pleading and begging him to stop. The more she pleaded, the more he got off on the beating he was giving her.

"Please mister I'm sorry!" Shay begged.

But her words fell onto deaf ears. He continued to stomp her head against the concrete, knocking her in her ribs and her back. She was starting to lose too much blood. She felt herself slipping away into an unconscious state. The last thing she remembered was the white man's foot meeting her face head on as she laid there unconscious. The trick ass white boy bent over, reached in her pockets, and grabbed his money back; unmoved by what had just taken place and the condition Shay laid there in. He hacked up some spit, then spit on her as he walked out of the hotel headed for his eighteen wheeler, leaving Shay there for dead.

As night fell, Bobby continued along a back road that lead out of Houston into Dallas. He was taking Weezy to the Grey Hound bus station where she was going to catch a bus into Bessemer, Alabama to meet with Hunter, one of Bobby's partners.

"Now remember, all you gotta do is act normal when you're at the bus station waiting on the bus. Here is your ticket." He handed her the ticket with the name Caria Simon on it.

"Once you get into Bessemer, my business associate will retrieve the bag from you, then he will take you to

Birmingham. There you will change your appearance by putting on these clothes that I have in this bag. All this is to be done at the hotel room that is waiting for you. After that is done you'll catch a cab to the bus station and purchase a ticket to Houston where I'll pick you up at the gas station two blocks over from the Greyhound. Now do you want your money now or when you get back?" Bobby said.

"Why wouldn't I want my money now?" asked Weezy.

Bobby handed her 25 one hundred dollar bills.

CHAPTER 10

A Hoe Into a Housewife

Winter had on a sleek, sexy, and exotic low cut V-neck red Armani dress, tailor made to fit every curve on her five foot four inch, one hundred pound frame. With matching red Armani heels, she sported a pair of one carat red diamond earrings that Garvin had bought her to go with her outfit. All eyes were focused on her as she stepped out of the super stretch limo that Garvin chartered for them to have a night out on the town in the Big Apple.

He had reservations for two, at the 40/40. The place had been renovated and tonight was the grand-reopening. Garvin had just cashed in on a multi-million dollar deal for the patent of a medical breakthrough in the field of plastic surgery. He sold his patent to a billion dollar medical corporation for 30 million dollars.

"I'm so happy that we are here in New York," Winter said as they entered the 40/40.

"I wouldn't have it any other way," Garvin said. When they entered the restaurant they checked their coats then verified the reservation for the night. Once the guy found their names, they were escorted to their seats towards the back of the restaurant. Garvin pulled out Winter's chair, then sat down directly in front of her. The waitress approached them and asked if they would like to order drinks while they looked over the menu.

"Give me a bottle of your most expensive red wine," said Garvin.

The waitress left then returned with his request. Then she asked if they were ready to place their order.

"What would you like?"

"I am still undecided, I don't know what I am in the mood for," Winter said.

"It's ok, I'll order for the both of us," Garvin said.

He turned to the waitress and ordered, "Just give us the chef's special for the night, please."

"So Winter, how is the life in the fast lane?" Garvin asked.

"What do you mean fast lane?" Winter wondered what he meant.

"I mean a sexy extravagant woman such as yourself? You should be settled into a nice home, married with kids," he replied.

"O am not the one to be tied down to just one man and the thing about kids, I like em - just not into having my own," she said.

"Now is it that your past relationships with men have made you bitter?" he asked.

"No it is not that, life just has too much to offer to be stuck with one man, that's probably sleeping around on the damn low! Where is all of this coming from anyways?"

"I was just concerned about you living your life without someone to call your own. I really do like you," Garvin said.

"Well Garvin, I like you too but you're married and I work for Stacks. He is my man, so therefore you and I are out of the question. Just because of those two reasons right there."

"What if you and I could be together?"

"Are you tryin to tell me that you wanna leave your wife for me? I'm flattered but I can't let you do that."

"No, I would never leave my wife, but my wife is leaving me. She is dying of cancer and has less than a month to live," Garvin said surprising Winter.

"Here is your food," the waitress said as she was setting the food onto the table. "Are there any more requests before I go?"

"No thank you, that will be all for now," said Garvin.

"Oh Garvin! I am so sorry to hear about your wife's sickness," Winter said.

"She was diagnosed last year a little bit before we met each other and now that she is dying spending time with you is filling that void. So I would really like for us to be able to get closer. Winter I've never needed no one as much as I need you," said Garvin.

"Garvin, I've been living this life style ever since I graduated from high school. I don't know anything but the streets and how to sell pussy. The only real happiness I know is the happiness of making Stacks happy. I've been hooked on streets drugs as well as over the counter drugs. Why would you wanna get mixed up with a woman like me, when you can have any woman you want?" Winter replied.

"That's just it, you are the woman I want. To me your inner beauty is as beautiful as your outer beauty. Truthfully there are countless reasons for me wanting you. Let's just start and finish by saying that it is said that Jesus married Mary Magdalene and she was the town whore. Jesus once said: 'he that is without sin cast the first stone.' He himself didn't even throw a stone when the people wanted to stone the adulteress. Now if Jesus can marry a hoe, then how come I can't?" Garvin explained.

"Who am I compared to Jesus? And I live in a glass house so I'll never throw stones. Now what else is there to say except for I love you Winter and want to take care of you. There is no need for you to sell pussy ever again. And if you just have to sell pussy then come be my forever pussy. You can have whatever you like. I want to be your man forever more."

"Crazy as all that sounds, truthfully, it is the sweetest thing any man has ever said to me. I don't know what to say...," Winter said.

"Don't say anything, just finish eating your food, then we can hit the dance floor, if you like, before we fly to Miami." He reached into his breast pocket of his suit jacket, then handed her a box with a ribbon on top. Winter opened the box and tears filled her eyes. Inside the box were two keys. One was the key to his condo in Miami and the other key was to a Porsche.

"Please accept these as a gift, representing us coming together as one. Now if you don't want this life I'm offering then keep the key to the Porsche and return the other key," said Garvin.

"Garvin I think the wine is messing with your head because if you think for one second I'm turning this down then you need not to drink anymore!!" Winter said with excitement.

"Are we going to have a problem with your pimp friend?" he asked.

"Who stacks? No he won't bother us, he has never forced me to stay but I do feel like I owe him a lot for everything he has done for me."

"So how much do you feel you owe him?"

"I owe him my life, but two or three hundred thousand will do," Winter said.

"So does this money go into the same account as before?"

"Yes, I still have that account number." she said.

"I keep all records of all my transactions. I'll do that as soon as we leave here," said Garvin.

"Then I will e-mail him letting him know what's up…"

CHAPTER 11

Weezy's Dilemma

Stacks missed the All-Star game due to the mishaps that were going on in his life. Shay was missing and so was Weezy. Winter had texted him telling him she was done with the life and the sex shop was not opening now because he could not get the permit from the city. The area was not a good area. Some sexism groups were protesting to the fact that it was in the downtown area and the laws in Texas were not like the laws anywhere else in America.

He was headed to the airport with LA to pick up Jennifer and Cream. Their plane had landed an hour ago.

"Aye yo LA, I was thinkin about selling the Estate and moving to Detroit. I think Detroit is ready for Stacks' pimpin," Stacks said.

"You know it's big money in Detroit bro," LA replied.

"Yeah I know this, plus I'm tired of Houston. I need a change of venue."

As LA pulled up to the airport, Jennifer and Cream were standing in front of the entrance that said PAN-AM. They both came walking up to the limo. LA popped the trunk and loaded their bags in. Cream climbed into the limo first, followed by Jennifer.

"Hello Stack daddy," said Cream as she greeted Stacks with a sexy smile.

"Top of the mornin,'" said Jennifer as she began to pour herself a drink.

"What's up? How was the trip?" Stacks asked.

"Excellent," Jennifer replied as she sipped her drink.

"I really appreciate the trip Stacks, I really and truly love you for it," Cream said with overflowing gratitude.

"Well it's back to business and as soon as we get back I'll be holding a meeting. But, in the meantime Cream, let me get some lip service."

"Must she do that while I'm in the limo?" asked Jennifer with attitude.

"You can always take her place…" he said jokingly. Cream was already headed his way. She started to pull his dick out for a suck and wanted to make it spit up. He leaned back and enjoyed the rest of the ride. By the time LA pulled into the

Estate, Cream was licking the head of his dick clean and was zipping up his pants, looking at Stacks with a big Kool-Aid smile on her face awaiting his approval as if it was her first time she had ever sucked his dick. She had heard so much about him dicking bitches down with his huge cock. She only wished she could have fucked him.

The limo came to a complete stop, Stacks and the girls entered the house, and he called a meeting immediately. "As everyone can see Cream and Jennifer are back and this here is Mercedes. Mercedes, this is your new family. I need everybody to start packing. We are moving to Detroit within the next week or so," Stacks announced.

"What about my schooling?" Mercedes asked.

"They didn't stop making Colleges when they made TSU, so you'll be transferring," he said.

"Where is Winter?" asked Cream.

"Worry about yo pussy not Winter, as you all can see the team has gotten smaller, so everybody need to step yo hoe game up," Stacks said.

"What about Weezy?" Pussy Cat asked.

"Do I look like I give a fuck about a lyin ass hoe, who played a part in short changing me MY money?" Stacks replied angrily.

"Well Stacks I'm not leaving until I can find my sister," she said.

"Look hoe! I don't give a fuck about you not leaving, because when I move, you move or get left by yourself."

"Ok Stacks, I understand," Pussy Cat replied.

Then he asked if there was anything else that needed to be talked about. Everyone was quiet so Stacks ended the meeting letting his hoes kiss his pinky ring.

This was Weezy's third trip to Alabama to meet with a guy named Hunter. She delivered him a suitcase full of heroin. She was not feeling this trip and she wanted to call her sister, but Bobby made her go and explained how much safer it would be if she didn't let anybody know where she was at or even speak to anyone. She was somewhere in Mississippi when the bus pulled over onto the side of the road.

"Everybody please remain calm, the bus has broken down. It just shut off and won't come back on. I called the Dispatcher and they are sending another bus. Just up the road there is a gas station and rest area. It's walking distance, so if anybody wants to go there, please go right ahead," the bus driver said to everyone over the intercom.

Weezy glanced out the window and noticed three unmarked cars on the side of the road as well. She began to panic and her stomach started to get butterflies. The Federal Agents got out of their cars and told the bus driver to exit the bus. One of the agents got on the bus, looked Weezy right in the face and said, "Wanita Underwood, would you please come with me?" Weezy got up and walked to the front of the bus. When she did the fed grabbed her by the arm and escorted her off the bus. She became aware that the bus driver was not actually a real bus driver, but he was a Federal agent. He removed her bag from under the bus and handed it to another agent, then they all walked to an unmarked vehicle and opened the door where the real Greyhound Bus driver got out. They then placed Weezy where he had been sitting in the back seat.

The driver got onto the bus and started it right up. Then the bus pulled away leaving her there with the Feds. She was taken to a Federal Holding Facility and placed in a private room, hand cuffed to the chair. A Federal agent entered the room.

"Hello Ms. Underwood! I am Special Agent Greg Hawthorn. You are in some serious trouble, that I'm sure you didn't think was as serious as it would be. You are actually in way over your head. Unfortunately for you, you are looking at a 25 year sentence for the narcotics you were transporting for this man."

He slid a brown envelope across the table to her, then walked up to her and unhand-cuffed her. She pulled out over ten different pictures of her and Bobby together. The first picture was her being handed money in the parking lot connected to the Denny's. The second was her with Bobby headed to Dallas, then there were pictures of her handing Hunter the suitcases in Alabama and she noticed plenty of similar pictures.

"Ok Ms. Underwood we have been trying to get this guy for years. It's just that he is too smart and nobody will testify against him or cooperate with us to get him convicted. Now we're not looking to bust you, but there is enough evidence on you that we can put your high yellow ass so far in prison that a person would have to pump air to you so you can breathe. Or you can cooperate with us and wear this wire and go on through with every move you usually make," he explained.

"Ok sir, please I don't wanna serve 25 years in prison, I'll do whatever it takes for my freedom," Weezy pleaded.

The feds wired her up, took her to a private jet and flew her to a stop right outside of Birmingham where the bus stopped before going into the city. They told her they would be watching her every move and recording everything she said and if she decided to back out or alerted Hunter, then she would spend the rest of her life behind bars. So she did exactly what she was told to do.

She then got back to Houston where Bobby picked her up. They waited until Bobby was back in Gavelston, Texas pulling into his driveway before they began to raid him. Hunter was also taken down in Alabama. The Feds had tried to get Bobby to turn on his connect. Bobby lived by the secret code of life. He wouldn't even speak a word. It was as if they had a mute dumb guy in their custody, even after the showed him the pictures, as well as the recorded conversations. There was no breaking Bobby. He knew they had him so he went down like a man!

As for Weezy, they promised her she would get five years for her cooperation, along with supervised released.

Shay came out of her coma just long enough to realize that she was in the hospital, laying in the bed connected to all kinds of machines with tubes up her nose and in her arm. The brainwave machine alerted the nurse of the brain activity. Then Shay slipped back into a coma.

Shay had been found on the brink of death by a pizza delivery boy who had the wrong room number. He knocked on the door and it came open. When he saw how the room had been totally trashed he became devastated by the lifeless body that laid on the floor. He rushed in to check her pulse and saw that she was not dead. He then called 911. The dispatcher told him to try not to touch anything and for him to wait for the ambulance and police to arrive outside of the room. He did as he was told and when the police arrived he gave a statement. He went back to work and was now waiting for her recovery. When Shay woke up he was in the bathroom.

When the nurses came in, with doctors, he was shocked by what they had told him and he vowed to stand by her side until she came out of the coma. He told himself that he would go to work and come back. He felt sorry for Shay and had a special connection with her because his sister died in a hotel room after being raped and beat to death. His sister was a prostitute, as well, and he could tell that Shay was a heroin addict like his sister by the needle marks in her arm. He felt responsible for his sister's death because he never stood by her side to give her support when she needed him the most.

His sister raised him since he was nine, right after his mother left for the store to never return home again. He later found out that his mother left headed to California with her boyfriend, who was a musician.

His sister was only 14 when she became a prostitute to support the both of them. Then she was introduced to drugs by her pimp, so as he got older he thought that it was his sister's fault for his mother leaving them. So when she turned to him for help, he turned his back on her.

Chapter 12

The Worst Kind of Betrayal

Precious and K were signing the last few papers they needed to sign so that they could close on a beautiful, overly expensive, beach house that sat on one hundred acres of green land and white sands. The beach house was located in Montego Bay, Jamaica.

As a child growing up Precious watched her mother take plenty of trips to Jamaica. It wasn't until she turned 14 that she took a trip with her mother to Jamaica that she realized she wanted to kick up her feet and live out her adult years there. Now her dream had been manifested in the early stages of her retirement from the life as a hustler.

"Oh thank you," Precious said to the real-estate agent as she slid the signed document over to her.

"I hope you two enjoy your property and in the future if you are looking to buy some more property or sell the one you have, please give me a call," the agent said.

"Have a nice day Mrs. Oruoho," K said to the African woman.

Then K and Precious got up and walked out of the real estate office.

"Well baby all we have to do now is sell the club in Ohio and pay Stacks back the money we owe him. Then sign over our share of the club in Vegas," K said.

"K, I don't wanna sell the club in Ohio, or let the club go in Vegas. I figured that we could just operate both businesses from Jamaica by hiring someone we can trust to run both businesses," Precious suggested.

"I thought that the whole reason for buying property in Jamaica was to leave this whole lifestyle behind us," K asked.

"Yeah the lifestyle, but not the money baby. The money is too good to let go," she said.

K and Precious flew back to Vegas to take care of their business affairs. As they were getting into the car K told her that he had a surprise for her. He drove them to downtown Vegas. When he reached the destination he pulled over, got out of the car, and opened the door for Precious. He grabbed her by the hand and told her to look up towards the billboard sign.

It read, "PRECIOUS YOU ARE THE LOVE OF MY LIFE, PLEASE DO ME THE HONOR OF BECOMING MY WIFE. WILL YOU MARRY ME?" Precious turned back around toward K, who was down on one knee with a ring in his hand and a big smile on his face.

"Yes K, I will marry you!" Then K slid the ring onto her finger, got up and gave Precious a big long kiss and held her close to him.

It was Wednesday night at the Strip club, which was ladies night. The male dancers were in the house doing the sling shot, popping dicks in all of the hot and horny faces of women of all ages. Precious was sitting at the bar observing the scene in the club when her trouble walked in.

He was a male dancer who went by the name of Black Kryptonite. He was a straight hood nigga as he walked in wearing all black. He was cut up with his muscles bulging out of his tank top. She watched him out the corner of her eye, as she saw him making his way over to her. All heads turned with each step he made as he was grinning, flashing his platinum diamonds that were blinging from the different lights that hit his mouth.

The closer he got the more she had a tingling sensation going through her body. She tried to play it off like she didn't see him coming her way. She didn't want to lose her cool like she had in the past, which had led her to letting him have his way with the pussy. The three times she did it with him, each time, the condom busted.

"What's up Lil Mamma?" he asked.

"I thought I told you not to come back in my club?" asked Precious.

"Yeah, you did say that and if I remember right, I thought I told you that I'll stop coming in your club when you stop allowing me to put this dick up in you," Black Kryptonite replied.

"Why do you act like you God's gift to this earth and that every woman wants to fuck you?" Precious asked.

"My name speaks for its self and I'm not God's gift to this earth, I'm just God's gift to you. As for every woman wanting to fuck me, I have no control over being able to fuck any woman I want. But right now, I'm not tryna fuck nobody but you," he replied. "You know that pussy is meant for this dick."

"Look Black, please don't do this, I am already feeling bad about being pregnant and not knowing if my man or if you're the father," said Precious. He ignored her then started walking straight to the back where the men's bathroom was, as well as the stairs that lead to her office upstairs. Precious stood up and headed in the same direction as he did because she knew he was not leaving without her giving him a shot of pussy. Plus it had been awhile since she had been fucked with the intensified force he displayed.

She had to admit K fucked her good and could dog the pussy the way she liked it to be dogged. But Black was 13 inches long, a lot thicker, and the way he fucked her was totally disrespectful. He showed no love, like K did. He would not only dog he pussy out; he would beat it up so good that when she would cum, it felt like she was having grandma seizures. Her juices would be squirting for at least a full minute. It was like she would be pissing out cum! Once she reached the back of the club, he was standing at the top of the stairs.

"Are you gone open the door and let me in or are you gone stand there like you don't know what time it is," he asked.

"Black, what is it that you want from me?" Precious asked.

"You already know what I want from you, which is the same thing you want from me. Some bomb-ass sex. That sex you can't get from that weak ass nigga of yours," replied Black.

"Don't disrespect my man like that," Precious said angrily.

"Disrespect?! Look who's talking, you probably pregnant with my kids and you got the nerve to be talking about me disrespecting yo man? I think the respect went out the window the second my dick went in the pussy," said Black. Precious smacked her lips and rolled her eyes at him as she opened the door.

Once inside he stripped down to his skimpy ass pair of black and gold bottoms, he stood there looking like a black Hercules, with muscles everywhere. His dick looked like a thirteen inch cucumber, bulging out through his underwear. Precious was sitting behind her desk as he put on a private show; one she truly enjoyed every time he performed. She had on a short mini skirt with no panties. He was moving to the beat of the music that was being played in the club. Precious quickly started pleasing herself. With two fingers inside her pussy she kept her eyes on him and his seductive rhythm. Her breathing picked up as she was now stroking herself, playing with her clit. Black moved up close on her, putting his hard dick up in her face. She pulled out his long, thick cock with one hand and played with her pussy with the other. He began pulling her shirt over her head,

"Ooohh baby, this dick look so good," Precious moaned. She was so excited about what was about to happen she completely ignored her cell phone ringing. She started kissing all over his dick with short, quick sucks, while he rubbed her breasts. She couldn't control herself. Not only was the sight of his big dick driving her wild, the Scarface/Capone cologne he rubbed on his body and ball sack was making her go insane. She was sucking on his nuts while stroking his dick, then she put the head of his penis into her mouth and began to make love to it with her mouth.

Her pussy was throbbing. She felt so good tears of joy started running down her face. He would never bust a nut, so before he exploded he picked her up and sat her on the edge of the desk, pushed everything onto the floor, then brought himself down to her pussy. He put his head in between her legs and parted her lips. He took a long sniff before he started French kissing the lips in between her thighs, using his tongue like a miniature dick with a super charged battery pack. It was a trick he learned at an early age back home in Highland Park Chattanooga, Tennessee. She was shaking out of control, pulling his face close to her as she tried to get away at the same time.

"Ooohh damn! You black muthafucka!" Precious yelled as she held on to his head as she began to cum harder than she ever had in her life. He stood up while she was having her orgasm, shivering and shooting her juices out of her like someone turned on a water fountain. Then he took total control over her body. It was as if he had put some Santeria Roots on her because she submitted to his every request. He put the bell head of his dick into her pussy, then started off with slow, long, hard thrusts. Then increased his momentum as he played with her nipples.

"Ooohh Black, please fuck me harder! Ooohh GODDAMN!" Precious screamed.

"Damn girl, yo pussy feel so good," he moaned. He was now slamming all thirteen inches of himself inside of her. Precious pussy gripped his hard erection like it was a suction cup. She was moaning loud, which turned him on more, then he leaned on top of her gripping her by the ass as he whispered in her ear.

"You love this dick," he hit her G-spot, "Oooh shit I'm cumming! Please don't stop! Deeper, deeper!" She shouted. Then he rolled her over and stuck his dick in her pussy with his fingers in her ass. She started bouncing her ass back and forth.

"Yeah bitch! I knew you wanted this dick!" *'SMACK SMACK.'* "Take this dick!" Black demanded.

"Ooh Black please fuck me daddy! Damn this dick feel good!" She said while she played with her clit. He was spreading her butt cheeks trying to put more dick up in her. Precious couldn't help herself, she started crying, thanking God for a dick that felt so good.

"Oh HELL NO! You cheatin ass bitch!" K shouted. He had showed up to surprise her with tickets to the Dominican Republic. He made reservations to a three day couples retreat. He stood there in the middle of the door as Black Kryptonite was slangin and bangin dick up in his fiancé and she was loving every inch of it.

"I can't believe you would cheat on me. This is why you never wanted me to come to the club on Wednesday night!" K said.

Black pulled his dick out of precious. When he pulled it out it was like someone had pulled a plug out of a hole because pussy juice squirted everywhere. He threw on his pants and

Precious clenched together her pussy and jumped off of the desk. She almost fell to the floor because her legs felt so weak.

"K I'm sorry baby, PLEASE!" Precious pleaded.

"Please what? What is there to say?" K replied.

"Excuse me bro, let me get past," Black said to K.

"Let you get passed nigga? I should be kicking yo ass," K threatened.

"Hate the game, not the Playa. I didn't rape that crazy bitch. She gave me the pussy. Plus there's still some left," Black said like the nigga he was. K swung trynna hit him in the face. Black Kryptonite slipped his punch, then came up with a left hook. Then with a right upper cut knocking K flat on his back snoring.

"Next time let that nigga know he don't own the pussy and the next time he interrupt me while my dick up in you, Imma kill his bitch ass," Black said to Precious.

"Just get out, PLEASE get out and don't come back here ever again! It's over, you hear me? OVER!" Precious shouted. She sat on the floor and grabbed K by the head putting his head in her lap while rubbing his face. K woke up and realized what happened, then jumped to his feet, searching for Black, who was long gone.

"Where the fuck did your boyfriend go?" K asked.

"Please calm down baby, he's gone."

"Calm down? Bitch you crazy. I just caught you with dick in your pussy, and enjoying it! Then the punk ass nigga laid me out! Imma kill that nigga and if you wasn't Stacks cousin and pregnant I would kill yo ass as well! The kids in yo stomach probably ain't even mines!" K shouted as he stormed out of the office….

CHAPTER 13

The Sting

Bell-Al Park was the flyest spot in the summer time in Detroit, Michigan. Niggas and bitches was everywhere in some of the baddest threads that had ever been seen. Stacks had to make his presence be known. He had LA set up a wet T-shirt contest, where the winner could win $5,000 with a two day all expenses paid trip to Cancun, Mexico for two. There were bitches in bikinis, g-string bottoms, and t-shirts with no bras lined up to participate in the contest.

All of Stacks' hoes were on the scene representing him from head to toe, except Pussy Cat who stayed back to support her sister who was still locked up preparing to do her time. Pussy Cat asked Stacks to put her up in a small apartment not too far from the Federal court house. She explained that she would still meet her five thousand dollar a month quota and send him the money through Money Gram. She stressed that she did not want to leave him and that she truly loved him for who he was; she just needed to show support for her only living family member.

Stacks had Akelia help him out setting up the festivities. He also had four Jet skis. He was allowing free 20 minute rides on them. Tequila had the grills going, making BBQ chicken, hamburgers, hot dogs, as well as fish and shrimp. There were coolers on top of coolers full of free imported beer. Everything was complimentary of Stacks.

He had a helicopter flying over the park in circles with a banner that read "PIMPIN STACKS," then the Good Year blimp flew over with the marque that read "STACKSONLINE.COM" promoting his website.

"Damn Stacks, you really did it this time!" Big Moe said, excited.

"Doing it up big is the only way I know how to do it Big Moe," Stacks replied.

"You know that Dolla D is coming by later on, after he close his shop up," Big Moe informed him.

"Yo, what's up with that ballin ass nigga Skeet? Is he still buying pussy like a hoe buy clothes?" Stacks asked.

"You know it!"

"The tripped out part is that he got more game than Michael Jordan had when he played for the Bulls! I think he get off on paying for pussy cause the nigga don't have to," Stacks said.

"Well if I wasn't married, I still wouldn't pay for no pussy. I just can't see paying for something you can't keep," Big Moe replied.

Tequila walked up and handed Stacks a plate with fish and shrimp, fries and baked beans.

"Get me a Red Stripe out of the cooler T-baby," Stacks asked.

LA came up to Stacks and told him that he was headed to go pick K up from the airport. Akelia asked if she could go along for the ride, but Stacks didn't give a fuck, because she wasn't one of his hoes, plus he was banking on LA knocking the bitch down. So they left for the airport.

"LA how long you been working for Stacks?" asked Akelia.

"Ever since I got out of the joint Stacks put me down with a job," he replied.

"Well the reason I ask is because it seems like you're more his friend than you are his employee," she said.

"Yeah, Stacks' my nigga, no doubt. I don't really have to work for him. It's more of a restrainer than a job. If I didn't look out for my nigga like I do then niggas would have to look out for me, because I'll be robbin' everything moving, layin muthafuckas down," LA said as he started getting excited just thinking bout putting some hot ones in a muthafuckas chest and taking the money.

"Calm down baby, I didn't mean to get your blood boiling. I was just curious," Akelia said.

"Yeah I'm calm, I just get a little excited reminiscing about my past," LA explained. "How I used to blast my gat day in and day out."

"I like the way you held shit down in Dallas when all that shit popped off. I just wanna thank you for that. I feel like you saved not only Stacks life, but mine as well," she said with gratitude.

"You're welcome. Think nothing of it," LA said with a little smirk on his face.

"Well I think a lot of it… and I wanna show you how much by doing this…" Akelia reached over in his lap, unzipped his pants and pulled out his dick and gave him a blow job all the way to the airport. As they were pulling into the airport where K was waiting, LA exploded in her mouth as she swallowed every drop of him and zipped up his pants and sat back up in her seat. LA came to a complete stop, then got out to help K put his bags in the back.

"What up doe K, how long you stayin?" LA asked.

"What's up LA, I'm chillin for a good while, until I get back where I need to be financially," K said.

"Financially?! You and Precious should be caked up, what happened?" LA asked.

"Yeah, Precious caked up like a muthafucka. But I just spent all my money on some property in Jamaica and put it in Precious' name as a gift because we was getting married until she did what she did," K said bitterly.

"Hey K, how you doin?" asked Akelia as K got into the car.

"I'm good Akelia! What's up with you?" K asked.

"Oh I'm ok! Why Precious didn't come with you on this trip?"

"Precious doin her and I'm doin me from now on," K answered.

As LA drove back to Bell-Al, Akelia and LA engaged in conversation while K remained silent in a deep train of thought, reflecting on the incident the day before between Precious and Black Kryptonite. He couldn't believe that she was that cold hearted to cheat on him the day after she agreed to marry him. K nodded off sinking into LA's butter soft leather seats. Ten minutes later LA pulled into the parking lot and woke K up. As soon as K got out of the car he was hit in the chest with a water balloon that was meant for the girl in front of him standing back up from just barely ducking the attack that the other girls were delivering.

"Excuse me, I hope you're not upset with my girlfriend for hitting you with that water balloon. By the way, my name is Lattia what's your name?" the girl asked.

"KayShawn, but everybody calls me K for short," He replied.

"So K, where is the lucky lady of yours?" she asked.

"I never said that I had a lady, so where do you get that from?"

"Well there is a ring on your finger...," Lattia said with a smile.

"The ring means nothing, it's there to keep the thirsty ones away," K said as Stacks walked up with Big Moe.

"K, what's good homie?" Stacks asked.

"Oh I'm just getting to know Lattia here," K said. Then he asked for her number, she asked for his phone and he gladly handed it to her. She programmed her number in his phone and then said goodbye.

"Where my cousin at nigga?" Stacks asked.

"Probably with that nigga I caught her fucking in our office at the club," K said.

"Fucking?! Are you serious man she did you like that?" Stacks asked as he shook his head in disbelief.

"Yeah that's the way she played her hand, the day after I asked her to marry me. I mean I spent all my ends on that piece of land with the beach house in Jamaica. I really didn't see it coming as hard as it did," K said.

Mercedes walked up to Stacks and told him she was going on a date and she'd be back in the morning. Then Stacks and everyone else enjoyed the rest of the day. When night fell everybody went to the Good Life night club and partied harder than ever. K was drowning himself with liquor, weed, and bitches. At about two in the morning Stacks left and went to the crib where he, Tequila, and Cream fucked themselves to sleep!

'RING RING, RING!'

"Yo what's up? Who this?" Stacks asked when he answered the call.

"Yo! It's me K. I need to holla at you Stacks, I'm downstairs in the driveway. Open the door up," K said.

"Man it's five-thirty in the fucking morning, can't it wait till later when I get up?" Stacks asked annoyed.

"Nigga you up now. Naw it can't wait playa. I got two bonafied hoes for you. Uncooked and they been asking for you all night after you left," K stated.

Upon hearing that, Stacks got up out of bed, went to the alarm system punched in the code, 34-27-8-11, then the electronic double doors came open. Stacks thought to himself, 'A pimp gotta stay fresh for these hoes!'

So he went to the bathroom, cut the water on in the shower and waited for the temperature to be to his liking. Then got in the shower to freshen up.

Tear Drop was the first one to step out of the car, standing five foot tall weighing one hundred and thirty pounds; all her weight was in her ass and titties. Her waist was slim with a cute face, she was a mixture of Porto Rican and Somalin built like a deadly weapon. Her hair was down to her back and ass that sat on a pair of sexy thick bo-legged legs that was being revealed by the short mini skirt with a small slit in the back. Her eyes were a beautiful shade of green. She had on a short sleeved shirt that was slightly unbuttoned low enough to reveal her cleavage from her sexy breasts.

K stood there realizing that as fine as these two tropical delights were, Stacks would have an early morning, putting these two hoes to work. That's when Butter a chinky eyed, caramel complexion skin with a nice wide set of hips that sported an ass stuffed in a pair of Apple Bottom jeans that looked like they were painted on with a pair of Prada boots hugging her calves, got out of the car. You would have thought her blood circulation was being cut off. As they entered the house, Tear Drop was amazed at how beautiful everything was.

"Wow! This is a big ass house," She said to her friend Butter.

"Well actually this is an Estate," K replied.

Butter was checking out the customized salt water fish tank that had been built into the wall. It was filled with all sorts of imported salt water fish.

She turned around and said, "Girl you ain't never lied, look at that Italian leather sofa in front of that wall to wall flat screen. He even got a built in bar with a wall full of liquor and expensive wines… not to mention this beautiful fish tank with all these exotic lookin fish in it."

Tear Drop turned to K, "Is it true what they say about the Pimp King being the meanest and cleanest pimp around?" she asked.

"Well I don't know, that depends on what you consider mean. I know he hate a liar and thief. One time one of his hoes stole five dollars for a box of tampons out the money she had made, to give him because she was bleeding all up and down the track. He took her home and beat her with the thinnest extension cord he could find for a full hour then filled the hot tub up with alcohol and turned the temperature on cold. Put the hoe in there and made her soak in the alcohol in her open wounds for another hour, the bitch was screaming and pleading saying she will never hold out ever again. All she had to do was let Stacks know what she needed and he would have gotten it for her," K replied.

"Rumor has it that he can suffocate, air, and drown water, all while counting his money." Stacks was listening now, standing at the top of the spiral stairs that sat off to the right of the living room with a high ceiling and marble floor. He finished Tear Drops sentence by saying:

"Yeah that's right! Just don't forget that I can make blood bleed and a hoe betta not get caught fucking around with my riches, my bitches give me my riches on a solid gold platter. That's why I stay so fresh and so clean. Ten hoes down for my crown better known as a muthafucking Pimp king a.k.a. the Big Dick Slanger," as he made his way down the stairs between the two females. It was Tear Drop that caught his attention because she was digging deep into her Louie bag pulling out what appeared to be rolls of money, Butter began doing the same thing. Stacks approached them all. K introduced the ladies who were by now standing there holding a hand full of money in their hands.

"This is Tear Drop and her friend Butter," K said.

"Hello Stacks," Tear Drop said while trying to hand him the money.

"Bitch didn't you hear what I said? My bitches give me my riches on a solid gold platter. Now follow suit and speak when spoken to," Stacks said. By now Butter had noticed the gold platter on the mahogany table and was putting the money on it, then Tear Drop followed.

Stacks went to sit down and told Tear Drop to go fix him a drink of some Puerto Rican Rum. He then motioned for Butter to bring him the gold platter. She handed him the platter and reached behind her back then drew her weapon and yelled:

"Get your hands up in the air and don't move! I am with the FBI!"

Before she could finish her sentence his door was knocked down and there were Federal agents everywhere.

"You are under arrest by the United States of America for the charges of White Slavery; Interstate Commerce and Tax Evasion. I have a Federal Warrant for your arrest. You have the right to remain silent...."

While Stacks was being read his rights the other agents were bringing Tequila, Cream, Mercedes, Cheri, and Carmela; as well as Akelia and LA who had spent the night in each other's arms, into the living room.

"Stacks I am going to ask you to turn around and put your hands on your head." Stacks did as he was told. The female agent hand cuffed him, then he was escorted out of the house by a male Federal agent. As he was approaching the black SUV the Federal Agent spoke in an angered voice, "Its guys like you that give a real man like myself a bad look. I just lost a daughter to a pimp like yourself. If I'm not mistaken you're the same piece of shit, and in the name of Brooklyn herself, I vowed to take you down!" Then he pushed Stacks into the back of the truck.

Chapter 14

Locked Up Again!

Stacks was arraigned a few days after his arrest. The judge denied his bail. Precious was in the court room with Kanisha. He couldn't believe he was back in jail, going through the same ole bullshit. Eating the same ole bullshit meals. Kanisha handed Stacks a paper that read "United States Of America –VS- Stacks Money" and then under his name were his charges. After reading this his lawyer said that the government was seizing all of his businesses and freezing all of his assets, including the money he had overseas in his offshore accounts. Then the Marshall explained it was time to go. So Kanisha stood up to exit the courtroom while they escorted Stacks back to Wayne County Jail.

Two months had gone by and today Kanisha told him that she would be to see him. She was staying at a hotel downtown Detroit. The guard had came out and got Stacks for his attorney visit.

The guard explained that he had one hour. Kanisha came in wearing a long dress to her ankles with no panties on like Stacks had told her to do the last time she was there. As soon as the door shut Stacks grabbed Kanisha and started kissing on her neck while she was unzipping the jump suit he had on, she reached down and grabbed his dick, bent down to suck it for about two minutes then Stacks turned her over and lifted her dress up and fucked her for the next 20 minutes real quickly until she came; then he busted off next.

"Stacks I have to say as of right now you're facing any where from 0-20 years if any of the girls cooperate with the Feds. So far no one has agreed to cooperate. I think they are going to try and get Weezy to sign for a 5k1.1, that way she can get her time dropped down, if not totally done with. The other day the Prosecutor mentioned it to the judge. Can you get word to her somehow?" Kanisha informed him.

"Yeah let Precious know what you just told me and tell her I said to get down to Houston ASAP. That way I'm good," replied Stacks.

"Now, if no one cooperates, then each girl will get one year and a day except Mercedes; she'll get probation for being a first time offender. All the Feds have is pictures of all of the girls with their tricks and pictures of you flying across the country with them along. All this will prove is that your business was not paying taxes.

Jennifer was arrested and released on bond. They are looking for her. They think she left the country because all of her bank accounts we emptied out and closed.

Tin was never arrested she says 'hi.' Now as for K, the only thing they have on him is a conspiracy charge, so if you beat your case he walks as well. But you probably will still be charged with tax evasion for your businesses. The guard knocked on the door and explained that their time was up and escorted Stacks back to his Federal holding cell where he sat in a deep train of thought…..

TO BE CONTINUED…………………

About the Author

Yasin abdul-mujib was born and raised as a Muslim all his young life. He studied at a prestigious all male Islamic School in Dewsbury Yorkshire England at the age of 11. He knew nothing of the street lifestyle until the divorce of his parents at age 14.

Subsequently, he experienced what it is to live the life of a non-sheltered child when he went to a juvenile detention home months after the divorce. This led him to living the life of crime, finding himself in and out of state and federal institutions.

Living the life of two worlds: one as a Muslim and another as a heartless criminal, he had the best of both worlds. It wasn't until his last "bit" that he started using his skills as a writer. He wrote a book, then more came to follow. Now as a writer and author he lives the life of a true "OG" to the game of life, reaping the benefits from the fruits of his labor.

Pimpasaurus

1. **Beat your feet** – Get to walking and go sell some pussy.
2. **Bonafied** – A thoroughbred Hoe.
3. **Burnt Chicken** – A hoe that's no good.
4. **Footballin** – Faking or Playing games.
5. **Fresh Meat** – A turn out or a new how that's green.
6. **Glue** – A hoe that has that, come back pussy that leaves a mufucka stuck on stupid.
7. **Hoe Down** – Get down with a pimp.
8. **Hoe pass** – when a hoe is excused for some dumb shit but pays for it in the long run.
9. **Lame** – A no-body or nothing.
10. **Killing Cash** - Making money hand over first.
11. **Maggot** - A low life pimp that's simpin.
12. **Main Line** - A pimps bottom bitch.
13. **Pimpadee-Mack-Pimp-Playa** - A nigga pimpin, mackin and playin a dolly darden out of her money.
14. **Pimpalicious** – Good enough to pimp.
15. **Pink Toe** — A White hoe or a snow bunny.
16. **Promoter** – Pimp.
17. **Reckless Eye Ballin** – Checking out another Pimp.
18. **Seasoned** – Up on game or been in the game with different Pimp.
19. **Simp** – Fake pimp in the game.
20. **Smut** – A nasty hoe.

21. **TD Syndrome** – Tender Dick.
22. **Tender Dick** – Fake ass Pimp; A Simp; Soft hearted.
23. **The Eyes** – When a person is embarrassed.
24. **The Stroll** – A street where hoes turn tricks.
25. **Trick** – A date spending money on sex.
26. **Tricking** – To buy sex.
27. **Turn Out** – A hoe's first time prostituting.
28. **Uncooked** – A hoe that's been hoeing but is not burnt out.

Stacks

...Still Pimpin'

In The Game

OG STACK$

www.ingramcontent.com/pod-product-compliance
Lightning Source LLC
LaVergne TN
LVHW051500070426
835507LV00022B/2858